SCINDE

OR

THE UNHAPPY VALLEY

SCINDE

OR

THE UNHAPPY VALLEY

RICHARD F. BURTON

IN TWO VOLUMES
VOL. II

SECOND EDITION

ISBN : 978-93-5324-353-1 (Set)

ISBN : 978-93-5324-355-5 Vol. 2 (HB)

First Published, London, 1851

Published, 2020

Published by

Facsimile Publisher
12 Pragati Market
Ashok Vihar, Ph-2
Delhi-110052
E-mail: books@facsimilepublisher.com

Printed at: G. Print Process, Delhi.

Scinde or The Unhappy Valley

Author: Richard F. Burton

SCINDE;

OR,

THE UNHAPPY VALLEY.

BY

RICHARD F. BURTON,

LIEUT., BOMBAY ARMY.

Author of "Goa and the Blue Mountains," &c.

IN TWO VOLUMES.

VOL. II.

SECOND EDITION.

LONDON:

RICHARD BENTLEY, NEW BURLINGTON STREET,

Publisher in Ordinary to her Majesty.

1851.

CONTENTS.

CHAPTER XXII.

CHAPTER XXIII.

CHAPTER XXIV.

CHAPTER XXV.

CHAPTER XXVI.

CHAPTER XXVII.

CHAPTER XXVIII.

SCENES IN SCINDE.

CHAPTER XV.

LECTURES AND PREACHMENTS.

"READING maketh a full man, conference a ready man, and writing an exact man,"—is a time-honoured maxim to which we now discount credence at sight.

Certainly it is a serious thing to oppose one's opinion to that of Bacon—the paragon of genius, utilitarianism and roguery. But, eminent doctors of the mind do differ on this subject, at least as widely as they do upon others; as they do upon all, in fact, when an opportunity for "differing in opinion" does present itself.

As regards the fulness produced by reading, you, sir, can oppose to him of Verulam an adequate rival, the sage of Malmesbury, who expressly opines that "if he had read as much as other men, he should have been as ignorant as they." I may join you, and quote a pithy Arabic proverb, which assures the world that those who dabble deep in manuscript are very like asses laden with many books.

One of the first things the Eastern traveller remarks, is how palpably inferior we are, and we ever have been, with all our boasted science and knowledge, in general astuteness, private intrigue, and public diplomacy, to the semi-barbarous people with whom we have to deal. History shows us that we have been outwitted by the Hindoos; we have been cosened by the Affghans; that the Persians, to use their own phrase, have "made us donkeys;" and that even the by no means subtle Scindian has more than once proved himself the better man in contests where the wits alone were allowed to work. Had we, you may be sure, contended against the Orientals with their own weapons, our cunning of fence would never have won us a foot of ground in the region of spices. Fortunately our strong Northern instinct, dear Mr. John Bull, carried us through all difficulties. When fairly entangled in the net of deceit and treachery, which the political Retiarius in the East knows so well to cast—our ancestors, Alexander-like, out with their sturdy sabres, and not having time, or patience, or skill to unravel them, settled the knottiest of questions in a moment, infinitely to their own convenience, and as much to the discomfort of their opponents. They undid by power of arm and will, by bull-dog heart, that—

—— Stolidum genus
Bellipotentes—magi' quam sapientipotentes,*

all the blunders of their Bœotian heads.

Having noticed a phenomenon, it remains to us to ferret out its cause. Our inferiority of cunning to the Oriental, is certainly not owing to want of knowledge of the people amongst whom we live, or to ignorance of their manners, customs, and languages. The Macnaghtens, the Burneses, and generally those who devoted their time and energies, and who prided themselves most upon their conversancy with native dialects and native character, are precisely the persons who have been the most egregiously, the most fatally, outwitted and deceived by the natives. This is a trite remark, but it cannot be too often repeated, too forcibly dwelt upon.

* "A stolid race, strong in war, rather than strong in wits,"—as old Ennius said of the Æacidæ, little thinking how remarkably applicable it was to the Ennian tribe, his own compatriots.

Does it not strike you that the uncommon acuteness of Oriental wits, may be simply the result of their ignorance? Instead of dulling their brains with eternal reading and writing, arithmetic, the classics, logic, philosophy and metaphysics, history, divinity, and mathematics, Yankee-like they apply themselves to concentrating their thoughts upon one point,—the business of life, its advancement, its schemes, and the terminus which it proposes to itself. Must not this sharpen the intellect,—sharpen it to almost a preternatural sharpness? Instead of collecting a mass of heterogeneous and uselessly valuable book-matter, in the shape of second-hand lessons and scraps of wisdom—"Orient pearls," when grains of wheat are wanted—they read experience from hard realities by themselves experienced, pondered over, and thoroughly digested, till each lesson and its corollaries come to be part of their mental organisation. Actual experience, you know, is to most men, "like the stern-light of a ship which illuminates only the track it has passed;" by taking thought it may be made to throw a long ray before and around, as well as behind. Instead of pinning their faith upon a chapter of Thucydides, or a leader in the "Times" newspaper, they, having no Thucydides, and no "Times," to lean upon, are forced to form their own opinions about passing events. They learn no wisdom from the Sir Oracles of their county or coterie. They trouble not their mental digestion with those modern sciences which may be fitly represented by a grain of common sense deep hid in a goodly heap of chaff—for instance, Political Economy. And instead of distracting themselves with the pros and the cons of a dozen differing pamphlets, they work out each problem as it presents itself, by the power of inference with which the knowledge of real life has provided them. Must not all this thinking work acuate the mind? At any rate the observable result of it is, that each man becomes as worldly wise a son of mammon, as his capacity permits him to become.

So—parenthetically to return to our starting point—reading, by which I understand our modern civilised European style of reading, may make a full man, more often makes an empty man by the operation of a mental lientery, and as frequently makes, for practical purposes, a foolish man.

Nature, with her usual acuteness, has set a bar, and a peculiar one too, to the progress of worldly wisdom amongst Orientals; the obstacle in question being their utter inability to conceive what "honest" means, to enter even into the lowest sense of the apothegm, that honesty is the best policy. Nothing poses, puzzles, and perplexes our Eastern fellow-creature, reasonable and reasoning being as he is allowed to be, half so much as fair dealing. For instance, you tell him a truth; he mechanically sets down your assertion a falsehood; presently he finds that you have not attempted to deceive him; he turns the matter over in his mind, hitting upon every solution to the difficulty but the right one. He then assigns another and a deeper motive to your conduct; again he discovers that he is in error. Finally, losing himself in doubt, he settles down into a distressing state of perplexity. You may now manage him as you like, *bien entendu*, that you always employ the same means. Truly said Lady Hester Stanhope—a shrewd woman although a prophetess — that "amongst the English," she might have said amongst Europeans, "there is no man so attractive to the Orientals, no man who can negotiate with them so effectively, as a good, honest, open-hearted, and positive naval officer of the old school."

On the other hand, if you attempt any kind of finesse upon him, the Asiatic, the fellow makes himself at home with you in an instant. He has gauged your character at once. His masterly mind knows what your dishonesty will be doing probably before you know it yourself. He has you on his own ground—he is sure of victory.

Thus you see how it is that many of our eminent politicals—men great at Sanscrit and Arabic, who spoke Persian like Shirazis, and had the circle of Oriental science at their fingers' ends; clever at ceremony as Hindoos, dignified in discourse as Turks, whose "Reports" were admirable in point of diction, and whose "Travels" threatened to become standard works, turned out to be diplomatic little children in the end, which tries all things. They had read too much; they had written too much; they were a trifle too clever, and much too confident. Their vanity tempted them to shift their nationality; from Briton to become Greek, in order to meet Greek on the roguery field; and lamentably they always failed.

So much for active dealings with natives.

When passively opposed to them, that is to say, when they are dealing with me, I would act as follows.

If they assert a fact quietly, I should content myself with believing it to be a falsehood; were they to asseverate, I should suspect it to be a falsehood with an object; and if they swore to its truth, I should feel and act upon the conviction that the falsehood is accompanied by malice prepense—dark and dangerous. But I should content myself with standing *en garde;* I would rarely attempt feinting at them; and finally, I would never try to penetrate into their secret motives, well knowing that there I should be overmatched.

All this may be unpalatable to many—particularly to those who have lived long enough in Europe, after a return from the East, to remember only what they wish to remember. Some have gone so far as publicly to express their opinion, that the word of an Indian is generally as good as that of an European. What a pungent, pregnant little satire upon civilisation and Christianity! The unprejudiced author of it certainly deserved to be avatared at Benares, or to be shrined in effigy over the gateway of Juggunnath!

The distinction one may safely draw between the people of the West and those of the East, in matters of *morale*, is this: among the former there are exceptions—many in the North, in the South a few—to the general rule, that "all men are liars." There are who would not deceive even with the certainty of self-aggrandisement, and in security that the world would never know the fraud. Amongst Orientals, though it might be unjust and unwise to assert that no such characters exist, you may, I can assure you, live for years, and associate familiarly with all ranks and all classes, and both sexes too, without meeting a single one.

"Charity, good sir, charity," I can read in your countenance.

It is a great virtue, Mr. John Bull, but a very cumbrous and expensive one for a traveller or a politician.

* * * *

Before we start from Hyderabad, I must prepare you, my good companion, by a short lecture upon the manners of the natives, for mixing with them a little more familiarly than we have done hitherto.

As every thing in the world has not yet been written about, printed, and published, in the East, we have nothing like "Hints on Etiquette, by a Lady of Fashion," or "Manuel de la Politesse," to learn from. You must not, however, conclude that ceremony in the East is an unimportant study. Very much the contrary.

The first thing Oriental people ask about you, whatever you may be, soldier, sailor, or civilian, is, "does he speak our words?" If the answer be "no," then you are a *haiwan*, a brute beast,—or a *jangali*, a savage. If it be a qualified "yes, he can, but he won't," then, by the rule of Omne ignotum, &c., are you a real magnifico. To shuffle over this difficulty in your case, as you will not have time to learn Scindee, I must represent you to be a Turk or Tartar, or some such outlandish animal, and declare that you are very learned in Ottoman literature—for which, by the by, may I be pardoned! Whenever any thing is said to you, you will be pleased to stroke your beard gravely, with the right hand for goodness' sake! frown a little, roll your head much with a heavy ferocious roll, and ejaculate syllable by syllable, Alhamdu l'illah, "Praise to the Lord,"—*àpropos de rien*. When a man shows you any thing admirable, such as his horse or his son, you will perform the same pantomime, and change your words to Mashallah, or "What the Lord pleases," (subaudi, "be done"): mind, if you do not, and if any accident happen to the thing praised, your commendation will be considered the cause of it. Whatever action you undertake, such as rising from your seat or sitting down, calling for your pipe or dismissing its bearer, beginning or ending dinner, in fact, on all active occasions, you must not forget to pronounce Bismillah, "In the name of the Lord," with as much pomposity as you can infuse into your utterance. By this means you will be considered a grave and reverend personage; *au reste*, by moving your head much and slowly, by looking dully wise, seldom smiling, and above all things by strictly following the Bishop of Bristol's "First Rule of Conversation"—Silence—you will do remarkably well for a stranger.

The next question our Oriental puts concerning you is, "does he know *adab*, or politeness?" here equivalent to ceremonial. You would scarcely believe how much these few words involve.

It is, I believe, almost always in the power of a European diplomatist sent on a mission to an Eastern court, by mere manner to effect or to fail in the object which his government desires. Manners, literally understood, still make the man here. Sir John Malcolm well understood this when as Elchi—

ambassador—to Teheran, he drilled his *corps diplomatique* to their salaams as carefully and regularly as a manager his *corps de ballet.* Orientals do not dislike our English manners, our brusquerie, our roughness, if it may be called so; but to please them, indeed not to offend them in deadly guise, it must be gentlemanly brusquerie, native and genuine, *sans malice et sans arrière pensée;* it must be "well-placed," not the result of ignorance, and not "antipathetic." Otherwise it is a dead failure, and the consequences of such failures in the diplomatic field extend far. For instance, we send to the most formal, haughty, and vainglorious court in the world a gentleman whom they were accustomed to consider the Boluser-General of the Embassy. The result is, that the sovereign considers himself slighted, and his ministers and courtiers are not slow to show it. The plenipotentiary, mortally offended, offends all by retorting with British bluntness and slights. He is repaid in kind; he repays in kind; and so on till the interests of his country are irretrievably ruined, and the goodwill of the foreign state is not only alienated, but transferred to a rival power. Another gentleman, brave, patriotic, and high-principled, but ignorant, violent, and strong-headed, is sent to settle certain nice points with the most savage, revengeful old chieftain that ever sewed up subject in a raw cow's hide. What is the consequence? Before he has spent a week at the court he seats himself in full Darbar with the soles of his feet diametrically opposite Majesty's face—a position as appropriate to the occasion as if he had, at a levee, presented his back to his own sovereign—he engaged publicly in a furious polemical discussion, and capped the whole by grossly insulting and abusing, in the presence of the prince and his nobles, a minister who, although decidedly the "most accomplished scoundrel in Central Asia," was nevertheless a prime favourite with his own monarch.

That envoy never returned to England.

Even in our humble capacity of travellers, Mr. John Bull, we must, if we wish to be comfortable, attend a little to what we ought to do, and what we ought not to do, in society. If we would not be thought "peculiar"—Orientals hate that almost as much as Englishmen—we must not "walk the quarter-deck," and set every one around us ejaculating—

"Wonderful are the works of Allah! Behold!

That Frank is trudging about when he can, if he pleases, sit still!" *

We must not gesticulate at all when conversing, otherwise we shall see a look of apprehension on every countenance, and hear each man asking his neighbour, whether we be low fellows, or labouring under a temporary aberration of intellect, or drunk.

Standing up, we must not cross our arms over our chests—in Europe this is *à la Napoleon*, in the East it is the posture of a slave. When walking it is advisable to place one hand, not both, upon the hip; or we may carry a five-feet-long ebony staff shod with ivory: this patriarchal affair provokes respect; a switch or a horsewhip would induce the query—

"Are they keepers of dogs?"

Sitting down, Turkish or tailor fashion—the most easy and enduring attitude—we must be careful to remain quiet for a decent space of time; if we move about uneasily every ten minutes, we shall not fail to hear the observation—

"Wallah! They have no dignity!"

And if musically inclined, we may hum a little in

* So say the Italians, "it is better to walk than to run, to sit than to walk, to lie than to sit, to sleep than to lie, to die than to sleep."

a low voice, and with a solemn manner. We must, however, avoid the main error of a great traveller*—whistling. Our native friends have no name for the offensive practice in their dialect, and the greater part of them being superstitious would probably consider it the peculiar modulation of the voice in which a white-faced man is in the habit of conversing with Sathanas.

Above all things, I say it emphatically, never let the word "woman" escape your lips. It is vulgarity, it is grossness, it is indecency.

Now briefly to describe the way of receiving visitors: premising that I divide them into three orders—my superiors, my equals, and my inferiors, for each of which there is an own and special formula.

Here comes Fath Khan Talpur, a grandee and a very polite old gentleman, with a silver beard, a sweet voice, a soft look, and a graceful bow. He sent a confidential servant† half an hour ago to inform me that he would "do himself the pleasure of calling," and I, after ascertaining from my moonshee his

* Burckhardt.

† If the bearer of the message be a man of no importance in his master's household, it is a slight to the visited, and must be duly resented.

fortune and rank, prepared everything for his reception. To have been "not at home," you must remark, would have been an insult. When the halting of horses warns me of the guest's arrival, I perform *istikbal*, in other words, I advance a few paces towards the door, to meet him as he dismounts. I then lead him into the sitting-room, allowing him time to shuffle off his slippers,* all the while repeating—

"Peace be to you, sir!—you are welcome—are you in health?—is your brain all right†—quite in health? *perfectly* in health?—And your family?—All your people?—All well?—praise be to Allah! Really I am joyful! But are you *sure* you are in health?"

To which he replies by smiling lustily, by looking violently amiable, and by putting exactly the same questions, interspersing them with such ejaculations as—

"By your goodness!—thanks be to Allah! May you be preserved!—I pray for you!—May you ever be well!"

I seat my visitor upon a sofa spread at what is

* To enter a room with slippers on would be like wearing one's hat in a London saloon.

† Meaning simply, "are you in good spirits!"

called the *sadr* of the room, namely, the side opposite the entrance, and seat myself by his side. Then both of us again seizing each other's two hands in our own, and looking lovingly, recommence the same queries, and reply with the same ejaculations. And be it observed, during the whole length of the visit, which, O horrible thing! seldom lasts less than an hour and a half, whenever conversation flags I approach my face to his, or he his to mine, and inquire anxiously—

"Are you *certain* that your brain is all right?"

So also, whenever the guest's eye wanders over the assembly of our united domestics, who are squatting upon the ground in semicircles, each on the side of the room where the master sits, exchanging politenesses, and at times slipping a few words into our private discourse, the individual looked at joins his palms, cants his head over, and puts the same question with every appearance of Scindee *bonhommie*.

Presently occurs a long hiatus in the dialogue. I then make a sign to a servant, who disappears bowing and noiselessly, then immediately returns preceded by my visitor's pipe-bearer, a part and parcel of the grandee's dignity.* We begin inhaling at the same time with

* Where only one pipe comes in, it causes a most tiresome Chinese-

polite bendings of the body, and we eschew the vulgarity of converting ourselves, as the Persians say, into Hammam chimneys.* After a few puffs I wipe the mouth-piece with the right hand, the servant raises the top in which the tobacco is, blows down the tube so as to expel any of the smoke that may linger about the water, and then carries it round to the members of the assembly that occupy the floor. The pipes appear every ten minutes.

During the process of inhaling, guest and host have been collecting materials for more dialogue. The language is Persian, Scindee not being fashionable, consequently, half the listeners do not understand a word we say. Moreover, Tath Khan, though a well educated senior, is not quite at home in the foreign dialect, which cramps his imagination, and limits his ideas to the one circle in which they are wont on such occasions to rotate. And this is an effectual barrier to the "flow of soul."

Observe a few small formalities:

Whenever my guest looks at and admires anything,

like luxuriance of ceremoniousness; probably five minutes will elapse before the guest can be induced to do what must be done at last—commence.

* Men who puff out volumes of smoke are compared to the chimneys of hot baths.

I say, "Pishkash"—"it is a present to you!" This is a polite act; to give an Oriental anything, even a flower, is deemed a particular compliment. However, he seldom accepts anything, because it is customary to send in return a present of much greater value.

Whenever the visitor sneezes, you remark, he says aloud, "Praise be to Allah, the preserver of the two worlds!" To this I respond also in gurgling Arabic, "May the Lord have mercy on thee!" an expression of benevolence which he acknowledges by a "May your kindness never be less!"

Another uncomfortable pause. This time I send for a little fruit, although I know that my guest's notions of propriety are too strict to admit of his eating it. However, he condescends to chew a few cardamoms, and perhaps drinks a drop of sherbet.* I am careful, you observe, to help myself first—poison, probably, made this practice a rule of Eastern

* "There are no three ideas which we associate more strongly with the two great portions of the East, than tea with the Chinese, and coffee and smoking with the Turks and Persians." So Leigh Hunt. I would amend the association thus, tea with the Chinese, coffee with the Arabs, and smoking or sherbet with the Persians. Many Persians will not touch coffee on common occasions, because it is always drunk at funerals, and so they learn to dislike its taste.

politeness, from which deviation is impossible.* So also, when he puts the cup down I do not forget to exclaim, "Hania,†—may it be good to you!"—he bows and returns, "May Allah be your preserver!"

Presently, stifled yawns and vacant looks become the order of the day, conversation appearing in fits, and as Barry Cornwall hath it—

"The voice of silence, sounding from her throne"

with imperative accents. Then my friend thinks it time to conclude his visitation. The first sign of our deliverance, is one final sally of—

"Are you convinced that your brain is all right?"

He then shuffles off the sofa, seizes my hand in his, and begins a series of compliments which must be answered by a repetition of the same. All his suite in the mean time start up from their squatting position, and follow behind as I lead him to the door. The camels, or horses are brought up to be mounted, my head servant holding the grandee's stirrup. And I, after a final congee, retire into solitude for the

* So you never ask your friend to eat anything without setting him the example, or show him into a strange place without preceding him, &c. &c.

† This is the Arabic word; the Persians say, "Afiyat bashad"—"may it be health to you!" or "Nush i jan"—"may it be a drink of life!"

purpose of recruiting spirits after so uncommonly severe a draw upon them. But I have my reward, I have won the old gentleman's heart. At this moment he is confidentially informing his confidant, who ere long will as confidentially inform mine, that I am an Adami—a "descendant of Adam;" in a word, a "man," in contradistinction to every Frank yet spawned; they being janwars, "beasts," and sons of beasts.

Politeness as explained by, "benevolence in small things," is all but unknown in the comparatively civilized parts of the East; as signifying mere courtliness of manner, it is carried to the degree of extreme. No old marquis of the *ancien régime* could bend a more graceful bow, or turn a more insinuating compliment than a common Indian moonshee: there is something so exquisitely soft, polished, and refined in the fellow's voice, gestures, and words, that he forces admiration upon you. No Italian prince with his well-assumed chivalrous bearing, surpasses a Persian noble in dignified deportment and transcendental ease. These two, Persia and India, having imperial courts, have ever been the head-quarters of ceremony. At the same time, there is much to admire in the manly simplicity of the Arab's manner, and even the martial roughness of the Affghan is not without a certain charm. Of all, perhaps the Scindian demeanour is the least agreeable. He wears a flimsy garb of courtliness, a second-hand thing too, and a poor copy of the original Persian manufacture: his natural coarseness is eternally peeping through the disguise; he is uneasy in it at times, and not rarely he is ridiculous.

There is an essential difference between the modes of receiving a superior and an equal. In the case of the latter you advance towards, not *to* the door; you address him in the second person plural instead of alluding to him as "he,"* and you carefully exact a full-weight return for every compliment you address to him. Odious is the dire necessity of being, from Calcutta to Teheran, perpetually "upon your dignity." Your visitor, despite his graceful salaams, his charming compliments, and his imperturbable ease, is ever striving to exalt himself and debase you by a nice and guarded slight. The insolence of a Persian

* This is the more polite and ceremonious address.

and the impertinence of an Indian know no bounds if you once give them the rein. As for coercing them European fashion, it is quite impossible. After a tirade of insults you send a "hostile message," what is the other party's reply?

"Wallah! they are miracles these Franks! The foal of an ass tells me to come and be killed! O his mother! Could he not have cut me down at once without any danger to himself?"

And the whole town will deride your outlandish ways in many odes.

If, guided by a ridiculous old proverb, you do in Persia as the Persians do, when you have been grossly affronted, you maintain a bland and pleasing demeanour, affect not to comprehend what has been done, and show your friend a little more than usual civility when taking leave of him: a wink at your bravo does the rest.* When undesirous of proceeding to extremes, you summon a stout "horse keeper," as grooms are here called, and direct him to insult your

* Not many years ago an English officer nearly lost his life in this way, in consequence of wittingly or unwittingly insulting his entertainer—a Moslem of high rank and nice sense of honour—by stepping over his hukkah snake.

insulter in the way you deem most advisable. Should your temper fail you, there is no objection to your starting up and seizing your visitor's beard, when, having him completely at your mercy, you may pummel him to your heart's content. This proceeding, inadmissible in English, is held venial, nay, commendable under certain circumstances in Persian, Affghan, or Scindian society. The world will say nothing about it beyond advising you to look out for a matchlock ball whenever you take your evening's ride.

By proper management these ferocious scenes may always be avoided. If the people know or suspect you to be deep read in their language and manners, they will be chary of offending you, because they expect a rebuff. Whenever anything like a liberty is attempted, you check it *in exordio:* for as old Sadi says—

> " One may stop the fountain's mouth with a spade,
> If allowed to run, it will bear away an elephant."

The best way to close your friend's lips is to reply by some fierely satirical remark, or to look at him as if you would bite him, or, if other things fail, to bring a forbidden subject, such as the wine-cup, or the pork-chop, upon the tapis.

In these countries the only social pleasure a man can enjoy is in "low society." You have no trouble in receiving your inferiors; you only arise from your seat or half rise, or move as if to rise, or simply bow your head as they enter. You may air your turban, unslipper your feet, stretch your legs, yawn—in a word do what you please before them. You may drink with them: in the presence of a superior or an equal, such proceedings would often subject you to a loss of reputation and the probability of most disagreeable consequences. If your inferior ever happen to lose self respect or fail in deference towards you, you take down your horsewhip and solemnly flog him; his mind at once recovers its equilibrium, he bows his head, owns that he has eaten filth and forgets all about it, except that he had better not do it again. If you leave him unwhipped his next step will be to play at leap-frog with you, or break in waggishness a long-necked decanter upon your head.

"Low society" in the East has few or no disadvantages. Your moonshee may be the son of a sea-cook, still he is quite as polite and certainly better educated than the heir of a prince. He bathes, he mangles no aitches, he has no radical opinions, and if he spits you kick him. The fellow may be a spy: he repeats to you all the scandal he can collect with the zest of a Parisian perruquier, and he displays considerable powers of invention in supplying you with tales which would keep a mess in a constant roar. He is in all men's secrets, according to his own account; everything, court intrigue, political events, and private gup,* he knows. Listen to him and laugh: only recollect that he makes no distinction between the *dicenda* and the *tacenda*, and that as he does to you, so he will assuredly do of you.

It is amusing enough to watch the laboriousness of the common Scindian's politeness. When he meets a friend he embraces and kisses him like an Italian. Then succeed a long shaking of a hand and a profuse shower of inquiries concerning his health and property—the cattle and the camels generally coming in for a reminiscence before the children and the family. To

* An expressive Indian word, now almost naturalised in the Anglo-Indian vocabulary, meaning chit-chat, tittle-tattle, small news or flying reports; concerning which the lady puts her first question in the morning to her ayah, the gentleman to his barber or bearer.

see and hear that pair under our windows, Mr. John Bull, you would think they were friends of ten years standing at least. Ask one who the other is, as soon as his back is turned: the reply will probably be "Bachho Thain (or some other such name)—a great blackguard!"

CHAPTER XVI.

WE PREPARE TO QUIT HYDERABAD.

One month is concluded. The cold weather is fairly set in. To-morrow, Mr. Bull, we start for a trip towards the south-east, down the Fulailee river.

We were comparative strangers when we first passed the grim portals of the Fort: now we say how d' ye do to, and shake hands with every soul in the three corps stationed in and around it: this circumstance seems to call for a little prosing.

You England-English do still in one sense of the word deserve the

"Britannos hospitibus feros." *

with which the pagans branded you. Let a strange man—a married one will be the best subject—betake himself to a little town in the old country, some Spa or watering-place in which "highly respectable people"

* Britons fierce to strangers.

congregate, and where there is no regiment to keep the minds of the community in order. The social atmosphere around him to him seems torpid, frozen, dead. The families to whom he has letters of introduction each number three hundred names on their visiting list, consequently they are not anxious to "extend their acquaintance." Those to whom he has not been formally recommended require a score of questions to be put and satisfactorily answered before they open their doors to him, even though he be a bachelor. Is he a member of the club? Does he live in a fashionable street? What kind of looking person is he? How many horses does he keep? To what county does he belong? Is he related to the Smythes of Smythe Hall, or is he the son of the opulent button-maker? and so on.

The residents, for reasons best known to themselves, have determined to consort with residents only, and imperatively demand from all candidates for admission to their "circle" a term of three seasons' stationary solitude at the Spa.

The visitors, after enlisting a sufficient number of companions in misfortune, bewail their exclusion and rail at the exclusives; but they are by no means hasty to extend the hand of fellowship to others in the same predicament as themselves.

The only chance the stranger has is to keep a dozen hunters, to sing Italian bravura songs, or to dance two dozen consecutive polkas, waltzes, and schottisches at each of the *soirées dansantes* to which he has had the honour of being invited. Then things may change, dowagers may become polite, daughters agreeable, the father may invite him to dinner, and the brother honour him by "dropping in to smoke a weed." But if his purse, his lungs, or his legs be not capable of such exertions, the stranger will most probably find the honest Britons very fierce indeed. Every bow will be equivalent to a bite, every look present a mild form of outrage: there is an affectation of fashionable superciliousness and a *guindé* attempt at exclusiveness, so painfully apparent that nothing but an ultra-lymphatic or phlegmatic constitution can support them for the continuance of the *trois saisons de rigueur*.

In India how antipodical the change—who would believe that we are the same race? Quite in the

"Come to my arms, my slight acquaintance,"

style, we seem to revel in our emancipation from

spa-tyranny and watering-place-oppression. Englishman or foreigner, in the service or not, with 200 or 2000 rupees monthly income; an ensign or a major-general, here you have nothing to do but to pay your round of visits when you arrive at a place, and lo! you know every one at once. If you stumble upon an old acquaintance, he puts his house at your disposal, you become an honorary member of his mess, you join the hunt or not as you please; briefly you are as much at home in a week as if you had been a year there. In some places where only a single corps is stationed, you have only to report your arrival, and by the rules of the mess, you receive an invitation to breakfast, lunch, dine, and pass your day with your entertainers till you think proper to march. Even in outposts, where no more than an officer or two is to be found, they will always do their best to receive you for the name and honour of their regiment.

But Hospitality is, you know, the savage virtue. Not that she seems to exist everywhere—very much the contrary—but civilized spots certainly know her not. Hotels and inns,* the circle and the position,

* Mrs. Graham, writing in 1809, says, "there is but one tavern in Bombay, and as that is by no means fit for the reception of ladies, the

have ousted her from the places where the polite herd congregate, have driven her to rusticate in country seats, and to hold her courts in the semi-barbarous districts of the Emerald Isle, and the wild parts about

"Thule, the period of cosmographie."

In India the poor thing is now relegated to the "out-stations." At the Presidencies you will meet her about as often as at New York, an English Spa, or in an Italian metropolis. Only that young India does remember there was a day when the family had a wide-spread reputation for keeping open house and for other similar displays of semi-civilized magnificence. More polished by furloughs and propinquity to home, than the rough and ready senior his sire, he has no longer the will—perhaps not quite the power—to keep up the honourable and honoured customs of the last century. Still he feels, (and 'tis something to have any sensation whatever on the subject,) and still he shows a little shame at the contrast between the "flourishing young gallant"—himself, and the "old worshipful gentleman"—his father. That is

hospitality of the British inhabitants is always exercised towards new comers, till they can provide a place of residence for themselves."

Now, in 1851, there are four or five hotels and inns; the observable effect of them may be taken in proof of my position.

to say, he does not desire you to make his house your home, but he generally has the grace to apologize for not doing so, and to show excellent reasons which prevent his indulging what you will please to believe the bent of his inclinations.

* * * *

This time we travel dressed as natives: there is nothing so intrinsically comfortable or comely in the European costume, that we should wear it in the face of every disadvantage. Young India—by which I mean young Anglo-India—would certainly wax violent if he saw us, and disclaim grandiloquently at our "morbid propensities" and our "contemptible sacrifice of nationality in aping Asiatics." At the same time he knows by tradition that his grandfather and father—who, to say the least, were quite as good men as himself—thought the thing no disgrace. You are old enough not to care much about what people say, and I have learned how largely we gain in point of convenience by widening the pantaloons, and by exchanging the beaver for a turban. Peasants will not run away from us as we ride through the fields, nor will the village girls shrink into their huts as we near them: the dogs will forget to deafen us with their barkings, and the cattle to fly in terror at our approach. Finally, when halted, we may escape the plague of being invested by a host of loud howling beggars and pertinacious petitioners, who insist upon the fact that such dresses can belong to none but Plutuses and Grand Justiciaries.

You have removed that strip of stunted hair which garnished each cheek—where did civilization go to find such ridiculous disfigurement?—your beard is neither black, nor long, nor glossy, but as it is, so you must wear it. I shall carry only moustaches: if you do so, every one will be singing of you

"The boy of forty scrapeth his chin;"

equivalent to remarking that you are a *ci-devant jeune homme* and *bien coquet*. Fortunately it is not the withered, sickly-looking affair that concludes many of the European faces which we see about camp: henna and indigo, oil and comb—you must not use a brush of pig's bristles here—will soon make this important part of you presentable.

Now, a few words concerning your beard.

You must not wear it too long. The people have a proverb that long bearded individuals are, generally speaking, fools, and it is an inconvenient appendage more troublesome than a wife, or daughter in her teens, requiring black silk bags to protect it from the dust and sun, oils of all kinds to prevent its thinning, dye every three days, and so on.

You must not clip it too short, on peril of being a "fast" man.

You must not dye it red, like the brick-dust coloured beard.—*

In cut and hue, so like a tile,
A sudden view, it would beguile."—

Of our old Scindian Moonshee. But he is a quiet old gentleman, with a leaning to clerical pursuits, and his chin shows it.

In conversation you must caress your beard with your right hand. If you wish to be emphatic, swear by it. Be careful in what sentence you allude to it: if you speak of anything offensive and your beard in the same breath, you will have committed a mistake, which men will not soon forget. And when you promise by your beard, recollect that you have pledged your honour.

In society mind to maintain the social status of

* In Cutch, some seniors are fond of wearing blue—sky blue—beards.

your beard as jealously as you would defend your "principles" or your political opinions in England.

If by any chance an atom of saliva from your friend's lips alight upon it, assault him incontinently. Also, if he speak of it broadly, impudently, without circumlocution, or in connection with entities which nature did not connect with it—tamely endure these things and you lose caste for ever.

If a man seize your beard in anger, you are justified, paganly speaking of course, in clutching your dagger and sending your insulter to "kingdom come" without benefit of clergy.*

If on the contrary, a woman, or even a man, in all the humility of supplication, apply the tips of trembling fingers to the "antennæ of your compassionate feelings," grant, if possible, the request for the honour of your beard.

Never apply the word "Kuseh"— scant-bearded—to yourself, or to others, unless hankering for a quarrel; and avoid to call a man "birish," beardless, as nothing can be more offensive than the insinuation it conveys.

* In Persia it is an offence punishable by law; even in the lowest ranks a man would be fined for pulling out the beard of another. The *canaille* in large cities seldom grow the appendages long for fear of rough handling.

When a straw or a grain of rice, for instance, sticks in your friend's beard, do not tell him of it bluntly, or pull it out, but look meaningly at him, stroking your own the while. So he will take the hint. Always exact a like ceremoniousness from him.

As regards the moustaches.—If you wish to be thought a Sunni, or (self-named) orthodox Moslem, trim the centre even with the highest part of the upper lip, and allow the tips on both sides beyond the mouth to grow long. Should you desire an appearance of great piety, you must clip and thin these ornaments till they are about the size of your eyebrows.

If you would be a Shieh or Schismatic, allow your moustaches to grow to the girth of a broom stick, in token of your intense abhorrence for the false sect that so vilely curtails them.

If you wish to appear a fighting man, a bully, or a hero, turn the ends up to your eyes, like a Spaniard of the old school, and twist them as you engage in combat. That is the wagging of the lion's tail.

If you would pass quietly through life let the ends meekly depend.

*　　　*　　　*　　　*

I make no apology, Mr. Bull, for the length of my lecture on beards. The man who ventures to travel in the East without knowing the use and abuse of one, is rushing rashly into many a rare trouble.

Now, Sir, of your toilette. You will be a kind of Turk, I a descendant of Ishmael, for the best of reasons—the characters suit us. I remove your black hat, the greasy "father of a cooking-pot," and direct your head to be shaved, excepting only a patch along each side, left to be "tittivated" and converted into "aggravaters." Upon your bare pole I place a cotton skull-cap, called an arakchin, or "perspiration catcher;" and round it I bind on twelve yards of sprigged muslin. It will be many months before you can tie your turban properly. Properly, I say, not like the ridiculous things in which the dowagers and chaperones of the last generation used to disguise themselves, looking, as to the head and face, exactly like the grim guards of an eastern seraglio.

Now, those collars—was the idea borrowed from the gills of a gasping fish?—must come off, and you may put your cravat in your pocket: it will be admissible when travelling, and useful to protect your throat against cold, heat, and damp. You must wear it however only when it is wanted, not always, which is ridiculous. Remember, Sir, we are not in a civilized land.

A muslin pirhan, or shirt with hanging arms, and skirts like a blouse buttoned round your neck, replaces its crimped, plaited, and starched European copy. A pair of blue silk *shalwars*, or drawers, wide enough without exaggeration, for a young married couple, the baby and all, tight round the ancles, and gathered in with plaits at the waist, clothes your nether man. Your coat is a long white cotton garment, in shape as well as colour by no means unlike the nightgown you wore in your boyish days. Then a pair of yellow leather papooshes, worked with silk flowers, a shawl by way of girdle, and in it a small Persian knife, with ivory handle, and a watered blade, equally useful for cutting your mutton and defending yourself from your friends—*ecco terminato* the in-door and summer *toilette*.

For winter it will be advisable to have a kurti or nimitano, a kind of jacket made of any stuff you like, from cloth of gold to cloth of frieze, padded with cotton, and sleeved down to the elbows. Over it again you may throw an Affghan chogheh, a camel's hair vest, somewhat resembling a Carmelite's frock. The very chilly wear postins,* (body coats,) or long cloaks, lined with sheeps' skin or Astracan wool. Handsome furs are very much admired in these regions; the expense confines them to the upper classes. Your cloak may cost you 40*l.* or 45*l.*: however as

"You have a Mrs. Bull at home, and many little Bulls."

it is sure to be most useful for the second generation when it ceases to be used by the first. For riding, I can find you a pair of top-boots—not exactly the dainty things that accompany "leathers" in England, but far more useful—a *chaussure* of soft yellow cordovan covering the Shalwars, and extending up to the knee. As overalls you have a still larger pair of drawers of coarser stuff: they cut like razors after a six hours ride, but as our marches will be short ones, you will find them comfortable enough.

Pray remove that useless circlet of base metal from your third finger, and supply its place with this ring

* These articles are made in numbers throughout Affghanistan; the largest may weigh from twenty to twenty-five pounds. The leather is tanned to a state of wonderful softness, and then intricately stitched and embroidered. The best cost from 6*l.* to 8*l.*; the coarse imitations made in Scinde seldom fetch more than 8*s.* or 10*s.*

of pure gold, with the silver slab upon which appears

جان بول

JAN BOOL.

the orientalization of your respectable name. Now draw a little surmeh* along the inside of your eyelids: 'twill make you look quite an Eastern. Your left hand upon the ivory hilt of your scimitar slung to its belt a little forwards, by way of hint; your right caressing the puce-coloured† honours of your chin. So, Mr. John Bull, now turn round and show yourself to the civilized world.

* Native antimony, used as collyrium.

† It often happens when the henna and indigo are not properly mixed and applied, or when they are used for the first time, they communicate a fine brilliant bug colour to the hair, more remarkable than ornamental.

CHAPTER XVII.

REFLECTIONS ON THE FIELD OF MEEANEE.

NEXT to the arrival at a "station," nothing more uncomfortable than the departure from one.

We ordered our camels to be here yesterday evening. They arrived this morning, and in what a state! One of them is ill; your dromedary has hurt his leg; two have torn their noses, and all of them have lost or injured their furniture. The surwans* are as surly as "bargees," and look as if they could murder us.

Not one of our Portuguese sober yet. They were invited to dinner by the messman of the —— regiment, a *compatriote;* the result is that none can walk, one can waddle.

The Moslems have, with all possible difficulty, torn themselves away from Bazar-sirens. And the Hindoos are in a terrible state of indigestion, the

* Camel drivers.

consequence of a farewell feast of rice and curry given in honour of them by their fellow caste-men.

It is a chilly morning. All our people, except the Affghans and the Hill men, look collapsed with the cold. The miserables have encased their bodies in postins, become Macintoshes by dint of wear; they have folded the ends of their turbans round their jaws, but their legs are almost naked, their feet quite so. Our pardesi * horsekeepers crouch upon their heels in a stupid state, and glide about like distressed ghosts, wrapped up in their dripping blankets, paralysed and wretched beyond all power of description. It will never do to leave them to themselves, or they will work hard to die of torpor. The only way to cure them is compulsory labour;—make them saddle the camels, hoist the boxes, tie the salitahs,† and trudge along the road as fast as their legs will carry them.

The first rainy day we have had in Scinde. But a year ago, Mr. Bull, how you would have grumbled at the prospect of this inky sky, at the depressing

* Pardesi, the "foreigner," is a name generally given in these parts of the world to natives of Hindostan Proper.

† The salitah is the canvass sheet used to contain the articles composing a camel's load. In cold weather it is converted into a blanket.

effect of the slow drizzle which descends with indefatigable perseverance, and the damp, shiver-gendering blast which scours the gloomy earth. See the wonderful might of contrast. You think the weather delightful: you enjoy the rain as much as a Persian* does. The murky prospect, so reminiscentive of the old country, here raises your spirits. Even the chill and the gloom have their delights after six or eight wearisome months of eternal azure and gold sky, and an atmosphere which feels as if lukewarm water were being continually poured over you.

Talking of cold and climate, I may hazard a few remarks about the strictures passed upon Quintus Curtius, an ancient who wrote a history of the reign of Alexander, by one Rooke—excuse the style of designation; it emanated from the conqueror of Scinde, and has now become classical in the province —a learned gentleman who translated Arrian. Curtius had indulged himself in describing the heat of Mekran, on the shore of the Persian Gulf, as very hot: of which Rooke remarks *tout bonnement*, "that

* Particularly the people of southern Persia, who enjoy nothing so much as a ride or a stroll during a shower of rain, which would clear the streets of an Italian town in five minutes.

the sun should scorch so much in a country so distant from the tropic, where its rays fall so obliquely, is incredible."

I can indicate an experiment which will show you what the glow is hereabouts, even in the month of November. Stand in the open air, with your shirt-sleeves tucked up for only half an hour; after a day or two the skin will peel off, as if it had been scalded or burned. During the hot season you may boil a steak, or roast an egg upon the sand in a very few minutes. Listen to an account of the sufferings endured by a party of seapoys marching, in the heat of the day, through Upper Scinde, by the pen of a late traveller:—

"A detachment of the —— regiment of N. I., escorting treasure from Shikarpore, were passing the desert in the night, when they mistook the way, and wandered the greater part of the next day in search of the track without meeting with any water to moisten their parched throats. One after one they dropped, until two officers and twenty-one seapoys were lost. The remainder, many of them delirious, found the track and a stream of water in the evening."

Affghanistan lies many degrees north of Mekran, yet the sun kills you there. Southern Persia and Muskat are situate within the same parallels as the country about Kech.* In the former, you find a burning wind as fatal as the simoom of Arabia; and the inhabitants are obliged to fly the latter during the summer seasons.

Thus much for the heat of "countries so distant from the tropics."

Again the sapient Rooke falls foul of poor Curtius, for his account of the cold in the land of the Arachoti. "What reader, by such a description, would not imagine them to have been under the North Pole indeed? I can assure mine they were very far from it, being then in a country which lies between the 34th and 40th degrees of latitude; and, of consequence, it could not be much colder than Greece or Italy?"

That consequence is a decided *non sequitur*. Hear Dr. Burnes about the winter, as it sometimes is, in Central Scinde:—

"While I was at Hyderabad, in January 1828, rain fell in torrents for many days, attended with a

* The capital of Mekran.

sensation of more piercing cold than I had ever experienced even in Europe."

The Rev. Mr. Allen, in Upper Scinde, found the day "so bitterly cold, that he appeared at dinner in his postin." Another "great fact."

And our soldiers were frost-bitten and frozen to death in the Affghan passes, whilst the Russians perished in numbers about Khiva; both countries being about the latitude of Greece and Italy; but not consequently quite so genial in point of climate.

* * * *

The field of Meeanee. There it lies before us, a broad plain, through whose silty surface withered stumps and leafless shrubs, rare and scattered, protrude their desolate forms. It is divided by the broad, deep, and dry bed of the Fulailee River, and is bounded on the left by the high wall of the hunting preserve, still loopholed as it was by the Belochies, and on the left by Meeanee, the little fishing village,* to which capricious Fate hath given a name in the annals of the East.

Of late years, sundry attempts have been made to

* "Meeanee," in Scinde, is the general name for the little villages populated chiefly by the fisherman caste.

detract a little from the brilliancy of Sir Charles Napier's victory. His despatches, somewhat too popularly written, were received with credulous admiration at first. In course of time they came to be considered, to be compared with private accounts, to be questioned, to be disputed. It is true, that the few present at the action confirmed their general's assertions; but, *en revanche*, the many who had not that fortune found out all kinds of disenchanting details. The princes were compelled to fight against their will; bribery and clannish feuds made our opponents more hostile to each other than to the common foe; the infantry was half armed; the cavalry commanded by a scoundrel in our pay, and the artillery worse than useless—most of the cannon wheels being secured by cords. Then the editor dashed into the arena. He told the world—"One square—one charge—and the whole business was settled." He remembered that at the time of the news reaching England, the late adjutant remarked, "the struggle could not have been very fierce, seeing that our loss was so very trifling." He concluded the flourish by informing mankind, that he "had no idea of the way in which the business was managed," and exited, exclaiming that Sir Charles Napier had "earned 27,000*l.* of prize-money with wonderful facility."

What delighted every military man who did not allow himself to be down-hearted with envy, was the way in which the brisk little affair was managed. Sir Charles Napier dressed his line at 11 A.M., unlimbered his guns, and began—not with charging cavalry at masked batteries, or with pushing a column of "murdered men" over a level plain, swept, and scoured, by hundreds of cannon,—but by silencing, as a common-sense man would, the enemy's artillery. An advance *en echellon*—a fierce *melée*, no quarter asked or given, on the river's banks when line was formed,—a dash or two of horsemen, and at half-past one the battle ended. The general's loss was 62 killed, and 194 wounded, out of 2800 men: decidedly not severe; discipline and tactics prevented its being so. But, in other hands—it would be invidious to specify them—the affair would not probably have presented the suspicious appearance, which at once caught the adjutant-general's eye.

The epoch at which the battle was fought set it off

in surpassing lustre. It was, to use a hackneyed phrase, the "tail of the Affghan storm," and most disastrous had that storm been to the lives and property of our countrymen, to the exchequer of the country, and, most of all, to the confidence of our conquests. The commanders of our armies seemed determined to demoralise the mass of them, the seapoys, by giving every work of danger and difficulty to the European regiments; * the seapoys, on the other hand, convinced of the little trust reposed in their courage and loyalty, and worsted, not through their own fault, in many a sadly-fought battle, had lost all that préstige of victory which makes the soldier victorious. Discouraged by their chiefs, they apparently resolved to merit discouragement.

Then came the battle of Meeanee bursting upon the Indian world like the glories of Plassey, the brilliant achievements of Sir Eyre Coote, and other dashing deeds which distinguished past from present generations. Once more 2800 thrashed 22,000 men, as they ought to do, greatly to the disappointment of certain old field-officers, lauders of days gone by, grim

* At Ghuzni, for one instance of many, four European regiments composed the storming party.

predicters, who "prayed to heaven that India might not be lost to us"—much to the delight of those who felt, as most soldiers did, that our fighting fortunes were under a cloud, that the said cloud was at length dispersed, and that the sun of victory was once more glancing gaily upon our bayonets.

* * * *

The battle of Meeanee, and another no less brilliant affair, which followed it, threw Scinde into our hands. It is the only one of the Transindine provinces that now remains to us.

A modern writer* on India remarks: "Our power which, since the days of Lake had remained inactive, like some huge Colossus, heavy with its own bulk, had suddenly made a stride which planted us in Central Asia." But the unhappy Colossus in question soon found Central Asia metaphorically, as well as literally speaking, much too hot for him. He remained there for a while, blind as Polyphemus, and blundering as pitiably; at length, finding that the new position had neither pleasure nor profit in store for him, he made a movement retrograde, blustering loudly enough as he went, but failing to conceal from

* The talented author of "Dry Leaves from Young Egypt."

his brother Brobdignagians, and even from the Lilliputians who had worked him such sad annoy, that he knew the retreat to be by no means the thing one boasts of.

Then followed the conquest of Scinde which, being an unpalatable measure to the Indians generally—who likes to live in a *mélange* of the desert, the oven, and the dust-hole?—was attacked on all sides. Every man with a tongue or a pen had his hit at it.

The principal objections to the victors' policy were two in number. In the first place, it was urged that the act itself was an atrocious one, that a quarrel had been forced upon the native princes, and that their ejectment and imprisonment were utterly unjustifiable, even measured by the elastic rules of political morality.

Secondly, it was asserted that the act was an unwise one, and consequently that it should be remedied by being undone; in other words, by restoring the plundered property to the lawful owners of the estate.

With the first question I have nothing to do, being ignorant of the law of nations, very little read in political morality, and detesting nothing more than political discussion—of all things, next to polemics, the most unprofitable and impossible branch of the science Eristike. The second point is more in my line.

The old warrior, who conquered Scinde, has never been a popular man in India. To the Indian press, his peculiar style of personality, and his habit of giving what is properly called the "lie direct," rendered his name distasteful in the extreme. So editors, and party-writers, many of them knowing little or nothing about what they were discussing, but all cunning in the art of appearing to do so, attacked the conqueror in his tenderest point, his maiden conquest. Every blow aimed at it they felt would come home to him, consequently they entered the arena determined to plant as many "stingers" as possible, and, to a certain extent, careless of fair play, provided they could make any play whatever against him. The favourite hits here again were two in number.

In the first place, "Scinde continues to cost, as it has cost us every year * since its conquest, some three

* "This (1851,) is the first year since 1841, in which the income of British India has exceeded its expenditure; the balance of from half a

quarters of a million annually—whereas the Panjab promises henceforth to yield from a quarter to half a million a year of free return." So much for the contrast between a conquest made in the former case without pretence of justification, and one, in the latter, which was forced on us.—The beauty of *ad captandum* arguments, as they are termed, is that, some how or other, they do win the herd's heart.

Secondly, that instead of preserving the Indus, "the natural boundary of Western India," as our frontier, we have deliberately tossed away all its advantages, and have placed ourselves, seapoys, and stores, in a false and dangerous position.

Scinde is an unhappy valley, a compound of sand, stone, and silt. The desert cannot be fertilised, but the alluvial plains which it contains can. The country came into our possession battered by foreign invasion, torn by intestine dissensions—each of its two dozen princes being the head of a faction—and almost depopulated by bad government. It is therefore an exception to the general rule of our Eastern conquests. Experience in the Indian peninsular has

million to a million and a half, which for ten years past has annually stood against us, is now transformed into one of a quarter of a million in our favour."

taught us not to expect the revenues raised by the native princes, our predecessors; here we may hope, if I mistake not, eventually to double it. True, our wants are not trifling—immigration on an extensive scale is not the work of a day; irrigation requires time and expenditure of ready money; and, finally, the influx of hard cash, which the country must have to thrive upon,* is an outlay of capital which rulers are apt to make grudgingly. Something has been done; more remains to be done; and much, I am confident, will be done.

The regenerator of Scinde is the Indus. As yet it has been the fate of that hapless stream to suffer equally from friend and foe. Lieutenant Burnes, its discoverer in modern days, magnified the splendour of its advantages to an extent which raised expectation high enough to secure disappointment. He made light of the "snaggs," easily remedied the "sawyers," and found that the disadvantages of having no portage calculated to shelter or accessible to vessels of burden, was "more imaginary than real." An "Indus Steam

* That the agriculturists may pay their rents in any other way but in kind—a system of raising revenue the most unsatisfactory of all, on account of its being peculiarly open to embezzlement.

Navigation Company" was formed in England, and an agent dispatched to Bombay for the purpose of settling preliminaries: where operations ceased. The public felt the reaction from enthusiasm and speculation to total apathy. The disappointed, and they were not few, depreciated the value of the "noble river" with all their might and main, as a vent to their ill humour.

But apathy and ill humour have both had their day. Now it is suggested that the little steam-tugs employed on the Indus are incapable of developing its resources, and it has been proposed to substitute for them the river steam boats of a large size, and on the American model, like those which have been adopted, with great advantage, on the Ganges. And lest the march of improvement should halt at the river, it has been resolved to improve the ports, to lay out lines of road, and to erect caravanserais for the benefit of travellers. Such measures lead to prosperity, especially when undertaken, not with a Napier's fitful energy, but the steady resolve of an Indian administration; even the deadly climate must eventually yield to the effects of drainage and the proper management of the inundation. The Unhappy Valley may ere long lose its character.

As regards our position being weakened by passing beyond the Indus: Scinde is, in my humble opinion, exactly the frontier we require. What can be more favourable than an open plain for the evolutions of a disciplined army? What more imaginary than the existence of "natural boundaries?" more fanciful than the advantages to be derived from a deep river, a line of rocks, or any of nature's works as frontiers?

The occupation of this Province should act beneficially upon our Eastern rule, in two ways—actively and passively.

Lower Scinde forms an excellent base for warlike operations, should they be required, against the nations to the west and north-west. Considering the question commercially, Kurrachee has already, like Aden, eclipsed all the petty harbours which, studding the neighbouring coast, form so many inlets for our commodities into Central Asia. Should we, in future years, imitating the thus far wise and politic conduct of the early Portuguese, establish detachments in forts and strongholds acquired by purchase or conquest along the southern shore of the Persian Gulf, it will be in our power to regulate the stream of trade in whatever way suits our convenience best. In the meantime we content ourselves with diverting it into our own channel. Kurrachee lies in the direct route from England to the Panjab and the north-western provinces of British India. It has not yet been made a depôt for the reception of military stores destined for that part of the country, but the measure has been proposed, and will doubtless soon be carried into execution.

The passive advantage we secure by the possession of Scinde, is simply that we have crushed and ousted a hostile power, which might have been, although it never was, dangerous to us, its neighbours. The fierce, hardy, and martial barbarians of the Hala mountains and eastern Persia can no longer consider Scinde their general *point de réunion:* unsupplied with the sinews of war by the lords of the low country, and scattered by the want of a leader to head them, a single regiment of irregular cavalry and the British name has been found amply sufficient to check their predatory propensities.

Another good which Scinde has done us. Every few years, Mr. John Bull, you and your household suffer from a kind of disease, an intermittent fever called Russophobia. And during the attack you became a haunted man. A skeleton sits before your roast beef, robbing it of all its zest, and direful visions, partly the spawn of distempered fancy, partly deformed exaggerations of a real danger, abstract from your usually heavy slumbers half their normal torpidity. At times you start up, dreaming of bankruptcy:—you rush to the window expecting to see, strange portent, a wolf at your very door. Such is the nature of the fit: when it passes off it is succeeded by the usual reaction; you laugh at your fears, you make light of the ghost, and you prose out many sound and sober reasons, all proving the phantasm to have been an "airy nothing."

But Russophobia is not based upon nothing. There is no reason why the West should foresee "Cossacking:" the East sleep heedless of the danger. Russia contains the elements of the power, if not the actual and present capability, to do all that Napoleon predicted she would do. She intends also to do it. It is not without reason that she has directed the whole force of her craftiness against the self-sufficient semi-savages of Central Asia, that she has toiled to supplant us in Persia, that she overruns Affghanistan with spies, and that she lavishes blood and gold upon the pathless steppes that stretch eastward from the Caspian Sea. Russophobia, I repeat, is no dream, it is a distorted vision of possibilities.

You open the map, Arrowsmith's or Walker's. You produce and fix on your spectacles. You bend over the page, and pass your finger slowly, very slowly, along the twenty-five degrees which separate the nearest limits of the two empires. You pause here and there, especially when a streaky, caterpillar-like line, which means a mountain, a huge white space dotted with atoms to denote sand, or the frequent words "Great Salt Desert," attract your eye.

True, Mr. John Bull, mountain and salt plain, river and desert, lie in the way—but what earthly obstacle is impassable to genius? Nadir Shah, an uneducated barbarian, with a few thousands of undrilled Persians, marched from his capital, forced the terrible passes of the Affghan, subdued all the ferocious tribes that met him, and reached Delhi, the core of India, how triumphantly, his loss—a some hundred men—may tell you. What Nadir could, others can. One of these days the Russian may think that the Caucasus has done its duty as an issue upon the unhealthy portion of the body politic: a small sum of ready money, a proper use of the blood feud, and a season of fighting in real earnest, will, despite the redoubtable Schamil, his daughter-selling heroes, and all their European sympathisers, put the colophon upon the hills of Kaf. Steamers on the Caspian can carry any number of men from Astracan to the shores of Mazenderan: the Persians, the Affghans, and the Belochees, instead of acting obstacle, would hurry to the spoiling of India as vultures to the corpse on the desert sand.

The Hour for these events is not yet come, nor may the Man whose master mind is to create and control them have appeared upon the stage of life. But to question the possibility of the occurrence, methinks is mere ignorance; to doubt the probability that such an attempt will be made, a dangerous error.

Should India ever be invaded from the west, Scinde in the hands of a hostile power might give us infinite trouble; in ours it would be an outpost of the utmost value. It would compel the enemy to fall upon our possessions through one route—Affghanistan and the Panjab. Fatigued, he must meet us fresh and vigorous upon a plain country, where his savage auxiliaries would avail him little, and where our men are, to say the least of them, as good as his. He can create no division by a flank movement on Cutch or Guzerat; our war-steamers secure us against danger from the Persian Gulf and the Indian Ocean; briefly, we block up all but the most trying and perilous entrances to India, and we place ourselves in the most likely position to debar our enemy, should he enter India, of all chance to return.

* * * * *

In another point of view Scinde is interesting to those interested in matters oriental. The Hala mountains, be it observed, are the ethnographical, if not the strictly geographical, western boundary of our magnificent empire. The Scindians are Indians. A very different race of beings peoples the rugged ranges of the Kelat hills, and the oases that chequer the deserts beyond. Here a collector may raise his revenue without perpetual appeals to the bayonet; a handful of Europeans may still awe thousands with the white face. There, is no revenue to collect, and had there been, nothing but steel or hemp could collect it.

The short and bloody page which our ill-judged invasion of Affghanistan has inserted into the annals of India under the English, reads one living lesson as to the peril of "territorial aggrandisement" in that direction. Would it irk you, Mr. Bull, were I to waste a few words upon the dangers into which we heedlessly rushed, and which overwhelmed us, because we were unprepared for them? "So don't do it again, dear," as the maternal parent is wont to say in concluding a domestic lecture, will be *bien entendu*, the giste of my garrulity.

In dealing with people like the Affghans, the Belochees, the Persians, or the Arabs, we have three great difficulties to contend against: namely, the effects of the national faith, the social position of their women, and the nature of their penal code.

Except in history, or in a few scattered tribes, there is no such thing as patriotism in Central Asia; its *locum tenens* as a bond of union is religion or bigotry. The Persian will openly tell you, that he cares not one iota whether Kajar or Frank walk the halls of Teheran, provided that, firstly, his priest, secondly, his wives, be respected. Popular writers on Eastern subjects, are prone to err in this particular.* With much poetical beauty they institute a comparison between Islam and the dead knight of the mediæval legend, who, when slain by a bolt, was carried by his charger over the field, causing as much confusion to the foe as if the rider's arm were still doing, as wont, the work of death. This is strength of simile, deficiency of sense. They universalise from the individual instance which particularly comes within the range of general European observation, the Ottoman Empire, and they blunder grossly, as observers who adopt such style of deduction do, and must do. Islam is still in all its vigour, fervent and deep rooted in the hearts of men—I am speaking particularly of the mass in Central Asia—as it was when it first sprang, Minerva-like, in panoply from Mohammed's brain; still retaining much of the ardent activity of youth, together with the settled strength of mature manhood.

* See a popular work by W. C. Taylor,—"The History of Mahommedanism"—published by the Society for Promoting Christian Knowledge. That author's simile and many of his subsequent assertions, as that "the spirit and vitality of the Mahommedan's faith have departed," . . . . "the very Mussulmans themselves confess that their faith is in a rapid process of decay," &c. &c., are intended to show off by contrast, "the recuperative energies" of Christianity, and its "principles of restoration within itself." This is injuring the cause of Christianity. False, partial, and specious pleading, fails in the closet, though it may succeed in a court of law.

In the early part of the present century the fanatic Wahabis of eastern Arabia made a movement which would not have disgraced the days of Umar. They arose with the same intention of spreading their faith over a plundered world; they failed not for want of energy or will, but because they lacked the means of success. Nations are now better guarded against these human typhoons: the war canoe and the bow are not likely to do much against the man of war and the howitzer. But still there is nothing easier than to preach a crusade in Central Asia.

The position of strangers and infidels in lands so teeming with bigotry and fanaticism, must be fraught with danger; their countless prejudices are so many rocks in our way upon which the current of events could not fail to dash us. In the presence of British equity the Moslem sayyid and the Hindoo sweeper stand on the same footing; but let the latter strike or insult the former at Candahar, and what is the result?* The priest returns home, tears his beard, dashes his turban to the ground, assembles his friends,

* I quote these circumstances because many remember its taking place in Affghanistan.

threatens, cabals, and agitates, till he raises a tumult, which if circumstance favour it, may end in rebellion and massacre. Most of these Levites might, it is true, be conciliated, bribed, and converted into spies upon their flocks. But what a degrading position, for the first nation in Christendom to place itself in—to rule by sufferance and purchased obedience! Many of them, moreover, like the Irish priest, are out of the reach of douceurs, because money is no object to them, and the rank they hold amongst their countrymen would be lowered rather than raised by the favour and countenance of their anti-religionists. These men are the most influential; therefore, the most dangerous part of the sacred community. Offend one of them, and there will be a "holy war."

To suffice occasions for which Koranic revelation forgot to provide, throughout the world of Islam, Rasm, or the long established custom of each country, is virtually admitted to an equality with Scripture. The inspired ordinance upon the subject of adultery has been found by experience worse than useless: but it is inspired; it cannot therefore be altered, although it may be transgressed. So in most

Moslem nations the men are allowed to take the law into their own hands, and summarily to wash out an affront offered to their honour with blood.

A few months after that Sir C. Napier had conquered Scinde he issued an order promising to hang any one who committed this species of legal murder. Abstractly just, it was uncommonly tyrannical. It was as if the Allied Army at Paris had denounced duelling, and in spite of all the prejudices in its favour, which made the proceeding become a practice, had systematically shot every man convicted of an "affair of honour." The sanguinary custom of the Moslem world overwhelms with ignominy the husband or son of an adulteress who survives the discovery of her sin; he is tabooed by society; he becomes a laughing-stock to the vulgar, and a disgrace to his family and friends. Even the timid Scindians every now and then were driven to despair by the shame they endured; a few cases might be quoted in which with the rope round their neck, they avenged their outraged honour, and died, rather than drag on a scandalous existence. The greater part of the community amused themselves with shrugging up their shoulders at the Frank's outlandish ways, and, discontented with our new punishment of blacking the offender's face, shaving her head, and leading her, seated *à l'envers* on an ass, through the bazaar, to be pelted and hooted by boys and beggars, made prevention their motto, the bolt taking the place of the sword.

Such could not be done in many parts of Central Asia. The nature of the subject, Mr. Bull, forbids its being *approfondi*: suffice it to say, that for many reasons were the fear of the scimitar removed, the scandalous scenes certain to occur would pass description. Then the *finale*—"the shame of the Moslem is broken," and "Allah will aid in the good fight against these accursed." The murder of Mons. Griboëdoff, the Russian Envoy to the Court of Teheran, resulted from the misconduct of his suite: a fair dame as usual being at the bottom of the affair. And in Affghanistan, next to the dissatisfaction produced by our diminishing the salaries of the chieftains that held the passes; and the intrigues of the worthless despot Shujaa, who incited his nobles to rebellion, with an eye to finings and confiscations, ranks, among the causes of our disasters, the universal discontent excited in the breasts of the people by the conduct of their women under the new rule. It was taken up by the priesthood: ensued a holy war, whose objects were plunder and revenge; and then, as the Moslems say, "what happened—happened."

Our punishments too, how contemptible they must appear to the ferocious barbarians that incurred them. The Affghan is detected stealing; he expects to have his right hand chopped off: we lodge him for a few months, in what he considers a luxurious retreat, where he can eat, drink, doze, smoke his pipe, and abuse the Frank in plenary animal satisfaction. He covets or appropriates his friend's spouse: instead of perilling life or limb by the deed, he knows that these benevolent fools, his rulers, will do all they can to protect him. Overheard blaspheming—a crime for which he would be stoned to death amidst the ferocious exultation of his fellows,—he now can laugh: under our rule sacrilege is not a capital offence. He commits murder, and is detected: he expects nothing but a horrible death—to be suspended by the ankles, and chopped in two like a sheep hung up in your butcher's shop, or to be flayed alive—one of the most excruciating tortures that human ingenuity ever devised.* Resigned to some such end he smiles when he is told that he is only to dangle for an hour at the gallows, without the prospect of being left there to feed the crows; or that he is simply to be shot without the preliminary of being bastinadoed till sensation by slow degrees is expelled his form.

The natives of Central Asia are to be controlled only by strange and terrible punishments. In the early part of the present century, that determined soldier of fortune, Mohammed, or as you learned to call him, Mahomet Ali, defeated the Wahabi Crusaders, and made himself master of Hejaz, the district in western Arabia that contains the holy cities of Mecca and Medineh. Immediately after the decisive victory at Bissel he began the work of intimidation by massacreing three hundred prisoners who endured the disgrace of surrender with the hope of saving life. But he was careful not to put them to death in a common way; he cut some to pieces literally by inches, impaled many, and blew others from the mouths of his cannon so as to render anything like a decent

* They begin by separating the skin at the soles of the feet, and then tear it upwards by strips till the sufferer expires.

funeral impossible. The sanguinary Ibrahim Pasha succeeded his father to the office of Executioner-General, and in 1833, the Sublime Porte added to the family, with other investitures, the command of the harbours on the Red Sea, and the privilege of conducting the pilgrim caravans. The Turks found difficulty in holding the newly-conquered country: they were abominated by the wild inhabitants because they shaved their beard, spoke a strange tongue, and freely indulged in military licentiousness. Assassinations became of daily occurrence, massacres of small outposts was the next step in advance, and the victors were beginning to fear a rise *en masse* would conclude the scene of their disasters.

A bright thought struck the Turkish ruler: he knew that it was conferring a favour rather than otherwise upon a Bedouin assassin to behead him, to hand the carcase over to its friends, and to allow every little murderer to be embalmed in memory as a martyred saint on earth, and become a blessed spirit carried about in the crop of a green bird in heaven. He had tried impaling upon a small scale: he resolved to extend his operations and to see what might be the effects of the novel and horrible punishment upon the minds of his hostile subjects.

Perfect success attended the attempt. The spirit of even the wild Arab quailed at the sight of the stake. They could endure the death, but they could not the idea of its consequences. The body of every malefactor was doomed to the hungry dogs and vultures; no holy rite could be performed over it; a last resting-place in this world was denied to it, and what might not happen to it in the next? So the stake triumphed.

I believe, Mr. Bull, it would be in the power of any military commander to reduce an Affghan, Persian, or Beloch province to perfect submission, to "turn;" as their phrase is, the "tiger into a little goat." Thus: A village I will suppose refuses to pay its tax and the headman sends you a polite message inviting you —dog of a Frank!—to come and take it. You bluster a little at the messenger with the bold broad face, to give your part *vraisemblance;* you make a few preparations for attacking the rebel ostentatiously as you can; presently something happens; you allow the project to expire in embryo. You keep your secret to yourself and smile alone at the altered manner of those around you. When the arrogant Shaykh * has determined that you are a Námard—"a no man" †—one fine night just as the moon is rising you find yourself with a few hundred horsemen quietly jogging on towards the village of Shaykh Mohammed. You reach it in due time, you post a reserve for fear of fugitives, and then carefully set fire to half-a-dozen huts in as many different directions. The wretches try to run away, you kill all the men of course, perhaps a few women—if they catch you they will pick out your eyes with their collyrium-needles—the rest with the children you either sell to make a purse for yourself, or, if generously inclined, you make Bakhshish (largesse) of them to your soldiers. You conclude by levelling the place with the ground, and by cantering your pet charger with the high sounding name over and across it that men may say "Verily he rode Ghurrawn over the homes of the sons of Yusuf!" And finally you erect, in memory of the exploit, a Kalleh-munar,‡ a round tower built of stone with regular lines of heads—some prefer the live bodies of prisoners—cemented with lime into the

* The head of a village, &c. † Meaning a coward.

‡ Meaning literally, a "minaret of skulls."

outer courses of the masonry: the Shaykh, I need scarcely say, occupying a position more elevated than enviable. After which, believe me, you will be pronounced every inch a mard (man,) soldiers will swear by you, subjects will be proud to obey you, not a servant but will consider you a hero!—"Did he not kill five hundred men in one night and burn their fathers * in quick lime?"

Mr. John Bull, it is needless to say that no British officer could be found to commit such enormities, and that, were one found, a worse than the fate of Haynau would await him at your hands. But, hating cruelty, your taste verges towards the other extreme—an unwise clemency far more cruel than wise severity. Some claptrapping journalist never fails to catch and dress up for your taste some tale about the horrors of the last siege, or the few acts of violence which soldiers will commit after the excitement of a battle-field. You read and believe it: it is re-told and

* This expressive phrase literally means that the progenitor is in the place of eternal punishment. If a man's corpse has been "cremated instead of inhumed," the opprobrious term, "sons of burnt fathers," would descend and adhere to the third generation with admirable confusion of the literal and the metaphorical. When you say, "I will burn thy father," you mean that you will make the individual addressed laugh the wrong side of his face; and so on. The phrase is not only expressive, it is also various in its expressiveness.

re-read till the General, if he be weak enough to regard "public opinion," in the form of press-cant, or an ignorant public's credence of it, is deterred from doing his duty, from acting as he knows he should act. This has happened so repeatedly, that the very Asiatics have learned to shape their conduct by its probability. When an Indian Chief gives up his sons as hostages to an Indian liege, he feels that the matter is an earnest one, for he is not capable of such Roman virtue as to sacrifice their lives for the good of his tribe. To us, on the contrary, he sends them with a light heart. The boys will be fed and cared for; possibly they may be educated to make useful spies: in the meantime, the father takes the field against us, as soon as he finds it convenient to do so.

Mind, Mr. Bull, I don't want permission to erect minarets of skulls, or to hang my hostages. But I think we may claim, and you should concede to us, some slight relaxations of prejudice; for instance, free leave to modify and proportion punishment to the wants of a newly conquered people, of course avoiding such barbarities as massacre and torture. I would always flog and fine where you imprison. I would never hang a man without burning his corpse with some solemnity, and when sounded about the probability of my taking a hostage, I would reply by a gesture, mutely eloquent, which questions the possibility of discovering a certain tint in my organs of sight.

* * * *

Allons, let us retire to our tent and indulge in the natural consequences of reflections, preachments, lectures, and all sermons ; you see where it is pitched : the weeds are of a brighter green, and the shrubs are a little taller than their neighbours: some hundreds of our fellow-creatures are thus doing their last duty to the "Old Parent." We will not mention this fact to our servants, if you please, otherwise the fellows will be seeing ghosts—O that I could catch sight of one!—and hearing goblins the livelong night.

How the jackals astonish one after a month's escape from their serenade; the moon shines brightly and the air is pure and cool—a state of things apparently much to the satisfaction of the Canis Aureus. If you peep out you will see the wretches now scampering over the plain, now stopping for a moment to bay, now again bounding off, springing playfully as kittens over each other's backs into the dimly lit distance. One greyish senior has taken up a position close to our tent, the better I suppose to annoy us with his diabolical yellings. The cry resembles, according to some, the screaming of a human being in agony; others liken it to the loud wailing of grief; in fact, there is no end to the unlovely similes which it has provoked the sleepless traveller in his irritation to discover for it. The French, if I recollect right, produced a series of mono- and dissyllables which strung together may be supposed to give an idea of the nightingale's note. Take these words—

Wah! wah!! wha-a!!!
I smell the body of a dead Hindoo;
Where? wha-re?? wh-a-a-re???
Here! hee-re!! he-e-re!!!

Pronounce the first and second lines as rapidly as your lips and tongue can move, Mr. Bull, emphaticise the "where" and the "here" by aspirating the "h" as an Irishman does when he threatens to *whip* you, dwell dolefully upon the medial vowel, and after a little practice you will pass for a jackal before Billy, your son.

CHAPTER XVIII.

DOWN THE FULAILEE RIVER TO SUDDERAN'S COLUMN. THE STEPMOTHER.

We must start betimes this morning;—sixteen miles before we reach breakfast, and fourteen more before we arrive at Sudderan's column, dinner, and bed. Our road liés along, sometimes in, the channel of the Fulailee, to which I must call your attention, as it is interesting in more points than one. The mean breadth is about 350 feet, here widening to nearly double, there shrinking to half that size. It runs in reaches, which seldom exceed a mile in length. The turns are sharp, and sometimes close together, acting as natural locks to impede the progress of a stream which, flowing uninterruptedly, would draw off all the water of the Indus. The soil upon which the stream impinges is a precipitous wall of stiff, thick clay; that opposite is as shelving as the other is abrupt. The bottom is a deposit of hard, caked silt, covered, in the parts where the channel widens, with long and broad banks of light sand, drifted by the eternal winds. Pools of nearly fetid water, some of them upwards of a mile in circumference, are very frequent; and as this is the season for the kharif, or autumnal crop,* there is scarcely a puddle within convenient distance of the bank which is not made subservient to the purposes of agriculture. In some places, where the fertilising fluid lies far beneath the surface of the country, sets of three and four Persian wheels have been erected to raise and distribute it over the thirsty soil.

The banks of the Fulailee River, even at this time of the year, are not everywhere hideous. The fields are for the most part parched, and no extensive

* There are two crops, the Rabi or Vernal, which is sown in spring and reaped in autumn, and the Kharif of contrary conditions. The former consists of condiments, as fennel, mint, red pepper, coriander, and cummin seed; intoxicating plants, hemp and opium; medicines, as senna, &c.; the dyes, indigo, safflower and madder; vegetables and greens, as garlic, onion, radish, egg-plant, carrot, turnip, sweet potato, country sorrel, spinach, and fenugreek; the oil seeds, with the exception of the castor plant, which is perennial; a few pulses, as Bengal gram, and chickling vetch; and the grains, wheat, millet, and barley.

The latter comprises cordage, clothing, tobacco, and sugar plants, gourds, and some kinds of pulses. In Scinde, as in other countries, the year is divided into Rabi and Kharif; the first extends from October to March, the second includes the other six months.

cultivation is carried on, but the number of hunting preserves gives an appearance of fertility to the scene; whilst the frequent villages and cultivators' huts enliven it to eyes full of the desolate loneliness which has hitherto haunted us. About the middle of May, the inundation extends to this bed. The first rise sweeps a body of water through the head, a signal for the peasant to wake up and be stirring. In a week the whole channel is flowing, and on both banks the cultivators are eagerly working to make the best use of the time allowed for irrigating their lands. At the height of the fresh the wonderful capability of the soil becomes apparent; the crops seem to grow under your eyes, and the plants rise to gigantic size. The country is covered, even where cultivation extends not, with a coat of emerald green, and the gardens, so celebrated for their fruits,*

* To enumerate them:—The green fig (the purple variety is rare) would repay care; the mango is good, but sadly requires attention; the tamarind is found wild and cultivated, as is the dwarf palm which thrives amazingly; the mulberry grows well, and might be tried along the canals and other places where water is close at hand; the Phulsa (*Grewia Asiatica* L.) is almost eatable; the plantain is generally inferior to that of India, still it makes nourishing and wholesome food; the apple is poor and tasteless, resembling the "summer apple" of England; and the grape is not to be compared with the produce of the cold hill countries to the north. There are limes and sweet limes, but no oranges; the custard apple and the pompelmoose are found only in the gardens belonging to

bloom with double beauty. Everywhere you hear the monotonous creaking of the Persian wheels—a sound which borrows a certain pleasantness from the associations of peace and plenty—and the shouts of the peasants goading their cattle, or hooting away and slinging clay pellets at hungry flocks of impudent birds. Near the towns and villages, the banks of these streams during the inundation are remarkable for their picturesque appearance. On every eminence along them are lofty, domed, and glittering tombs, shrined in little emerald casings of mimosa, acacia, and jujube. Here and there are idle groups, dressed in the gayest colours, sitting upon the bank and watching the crowds of male and female bathers that people the stream. Busy throngs are to be seen at every ferry, and morning and evening long herds of cattle pass over by the different fords.

The Fulailee is the main artery of Middle Scinde. It has been asserted, principally, I believe, on the

the Hyderabad princes, and the guava and rose apple are almost equally rare. The cocoa palm has lately been introduced; it might be profitably cultivated on the salt soil near Kurrachee. The fruit of the wood apple is eaten, and the rind is made into snuff-boxes. The list concludes with pomegranates, (bad and stony,) varieties of the Sepistan or Cordia, and the jujube (*Zizyphus vulgaris*).

authority of natives, that it was one of the provisional beds of the Indus during the migration of that stream from West to East. But the fact of such shiftings has not yet been established, and, *en passant*, I may remark, that, if every broad and deep channel in this part of the country be allowed to claim the honour of having once contained the "Classic," we shall see ample reasons for supposing that that stream must some time or other have flowed through almost every mile of Scinde.

* * * *

You see yon long forest fenced round with mud walls and strong thorny hedges, over which appear the tangled tops of many trees, tamarisk and poplar being the chief varieties. There is no partition between it and the river, which advances a step every inundation, as you may perceive by the large trunks, which, loosened from the banks, have sunk into the bed, and now lie across it like scattered fragments of cyclopean *chevaux de frise*.

These Shikargahs, or "hunting places,"—Belá, as the people call them—form a peculiar feature in the face of Scinde. They generally occupy the margin of some wide stream, whose waters are dispersed through them by a network of drains, cuts, and ditches; thus they engross the most fertile and valuable soil in the province.* All the Shikargahs are government land, and the rulers' absorbing passion for field sports induced them to lavish large sums upon them, and to preserve them with peculiar care. "We value them," said one of the lords, "as much as our wives and children,"—a blunt truth which has been recorded by every writer that hath written upon the subject of Scinde, as proof positive of the desperate state in which those lords' minds, morals, and domestic affections must have been. Stripping the thing of its oriental exaggeration, you will come to the conclusion that the good Beloochis, like English country gentlemen, attached, peradventure, a trifle too much importance to the inviolability of their covers, and that, not unlike an angry duke in the North country, they were disposed actively to resent trespassing. True, they were sometimes barbarous in their endeavours to deter Robin Hoods and Little Johns from playing pranks beneath the greenwood tree. If you

* The Ameers calculated that every head of deer killed cost them 80*l.*, and our authors consider this no exaggeration, duly estimating the loss of revenue occasioned by converting valuable land into hunting forests.

blame them, Mr. Bull, you have only to turn over a page in the volume of your family records. Probably you have not forgotten—for it is within your memory—that a "learned" judge, a Christian and a civilised man, hung an unhappy poacher because he happened to cut a keeper's hand with a knife, drawn in a sudden fray.

Unfortunately for the princes of Scinde these preserves were as odious to us as they were dear to them. We found that "snaggs" come not from the mountains, but out of the Shikargahs. We required "a clear belt of twelve yards wide between forest and the river," to form a pathway for trackers. We determined that our steamers must be supplied with fuel, and that fuel was to be procured only from the Shikargahs. The owners refused, objected, and wrangled, declaring that we were about to ruin their preserves. We pointed out to them the finger of Providence tracing the course of events, whereby was meant that we *must* have what we wanted; moreover that this was the punishment for taking Shikargahs to their bosoms instead of wives, laying waste villages to make Shikargahs, &c. The men in possession again refused, objected, and wrangled, and yielded:

your steady resolve, Mr. Bull, as usual, carried the day.

You never admired *battues*, sir, and what is more, you never will admire them. You (I particularise the word, for your Cymbrian kinsfolk will occasionally fall, like Frenchmen or Italians, in bodies of twelve upon one, and your Hybernian neighbours show a little too much gusto in "potting" an enemy from behind a hedge) are the only human being in whom the principle of fair play seems innate. You limit it not to affairs between man and man, you extend it even to feathered bipeds and quadrupeds; consequently, you look upon the *battue*, fashionable, foreign, and even German though the diversion be, with no favouring eye.

For the same reason you will not admire the Scinde Ameers' sportsmanship. The animals were driven out of the thick covers which concealed them by a vast circle of yelling beaters and dogs, gradually narrowing, into a square or parallelogram, carefully staked round, wattled and hedged in to prevent their escape: this inclosed space was divided into irregular triangles, by narrow alleys cut through the bushes and copses in every direction, all converging to the grass hut in which the prince, habited in a green gown, was seated. There, mounted on a low platform, he awaited the droves of wild boar and hog, deer, black buck, and antelope, thronging and jostling one another in their terror down the open lanes. The sport was mere slaughter, firing into a wall of beasts ten or twenty yards distant. The only chance of a miss was when some frightened brute, bounding high in the air, required a snap shot to bring him down before he got out of sight in the cover. In some Shikargahs, when a grand hunt was ordered, the supply of water was cut off for a few days, and after the guns had been stationed in positions commanding the courses, these were opened to herds that rushed down to slake their thirst and be butchered.

The Ameer enjoyed all the pleasures of the field: his followers had all the disagreeables and the dangers. His son or nephew was expected to stand by him, not shooting, but exclaiming "Bravo!" at every shot the senior made. When told to fire—a rare honour—he never dared ascribe success to his own matchlock: * it was his father's or uncle's bullet,

* Matchlocks were generally, English rifles rarely, used.

still in its barrel, that had killed the animal. On the rare occasion when a tiger* was started, the Beloch huntsman, instead of leaving it to be dealt with by the prince, pressed forward with his trusty hound, and armed merely with a sword and shield, or possibly a bamboo spear, never hesitated to attack the beast, or, if he slew it, to accord to his liege the honour of the deed. Often the poor fellows lost their lives in these gallant, unequal encounters; often torn and gnawed they dragged themselves to die at their master's feet, expending their last breath to praise his prowess. A paltry shawl thrown over their necks was their sole, at the same time their sufficient, reward. When an accident happened it was sure to be followed by another—one fool makes many—and the people only loved the prince the more for thus permitting his subjects to die for him almost gratis.

These *battues* were the reverse of blessings to the country. The Ameer would sometimes spend weeks at the rural palace adjoining a favourite preserve, and, as in the royal progress of our early kings, his

* These beasts, rare in Central and Lower Scinde, are frequently found in the north, where they stray down from the jungly forests that line the banks of the Upper Indus.

retinue, which resembled a small army, quartered itself upon the villages around, and of course never paid a pice for board and lodging. The peasant that ventured to complain was very likely to lose his ears: even had he deserted his home—the *ultima ratio pauperum* in these regions—the step would have been considered high treason. So the wretches stuck to their hearths, and looked calmly at desolation gathering about them. Like a Persian soldier, the Scindian or Beloch retainer would never hesitate to pull down a house if he wanted a stick, to kill a cow for a beefsteak, or to slaughter all the inmates of a hencoop with his horsewhip till he found a fat chicken. The Ryots were required to act as beaters in hundreds, no matter how urgently their presence might be required elsewhere. The Hindoo was forced from his shop, the Moslem from his plough: they received no remuneration, and when their legs were ripped up by a boar, or their backs gored by a buck, a trifling present was expected to pay for all damage. These progresses also acted as active diffusers of vice. After hunting, the Ameer would amuse himself with listening to story-tellers, poets, and nautch women, and the scenes of debauchery enacted by his dissolute followers were most prejudicial to the simple peasantry, their spectators, and too often their imitators.

* * * *

Hoosree, a large straggling village on the left bank of the Fulailee—interesting to us for no other reason than that we break our fast here. We find an attempt at a Traveller's Bungalow, a mud house in the usual style, two loose boxes for rooms, and a verandah, the whole so securely walled round that you feel yourself, as it were, in an uncomfortably large grave. Some Englishmen delight in thus isolating themselves from the sable and tawny members of their species. For my part, I infinitely prefer to be in a place where one can be giggled at by the young, and scowled at by the old ladies, as they pass to and from the well; where one can throw sugar-plums to, and watch the passions thereby called into being from, sweet, innocent, and artless childhood; where we can excite the men by sketching them, and showing them the caricature; startle the greybeard by disputing his dogmas; and wrangle about theology with the angry beggars.* Our turbans

* In these countries all beggars, Moslems as Hindoos, may be looked

will preserve us from the dignified uneasiness that besets the hatted head. The people can easily perceive by our hog-skin saddles, our English bridles, the chairs upon which we sit at meals, and our using such ridiculous implements as forks and spoons, when nature supplied us with fingers and palms, that we are strange men. Still we do not startle them. They are beginning to feel easy in the presence of European-aping natives from Bombay and Delhi—dark officers, who wear white kid gloves when promenading, and shake hands with the ladies—moonshees in pagris and angarkhas* above, British pantaloons and patent leather boots below—and half-castes, who hopelessly essay to imitate the ruling race by a bellowing voice, short hair, and a free use of milk of roses. To this hybrid offspring of civilisation and barbarism they are, I repeat, so accustomed, that they look upon us only as some hitherto unseen variety of the species; and in their curiosity they press forward eagerly, as you have done, sir, to find yourself face to face with an infant elephant, or an

upon in the light of mendicant friars, or "holy limitoures," for they invariably have a smattering of divinity, belong to some religious order, and idle away their time in the name of the Lord.

* The pagri is the turban; the angarkha a long coat of white cotton.

ourang-outang marvellous for hideousness. As we pass out of the stifling bungalow towards the rowtie,* pitched by order under the shady jujube trees, remark, if you please, the want of windows and doors in the "hostelry," how typical of the state of a newly-conquered country, governed by a ready and vigorous hand.

When, Mr. John Bull, will you be able to live at home and dispense with lock and chain? When do you think we shall again enjoy that luxury in districts which, like Bengal Proper and other places, you have disordered with your Civil Codes and Supreme Courts?

About the advent time of the Greek Kalends!

Here this admirable state of security will linger in the country parts till the province become thoroughly "assimilated" to the rule of British India, and the people grow familiar with the white-faced man and the fond folly of his justice-ideas. Then, as in Guzerat and Kattywar, we shall be cut down on the high road, or stabbed in our tents, or poisoned in our houses, and be generally liable to be plundered and beaten at home and abroad. And then, sir, you will stolidly wonder how it is? You will, perhaps,

* The smallest kind of tent used for servants.

especially if Billy your eldest come to an untimely end in some roadside fray, talk of sending out a Commission to enquire into the cause of existing evils.—

Listen, sir, I must repeat a very old truth to you. A military government is the only form of legislature precisely adapted to these countries.

Well, Mr. Bull, I know it! You hate a rule of soldiers. You would be upon the verge of insanity were a red coat to arrest you: you scarcely grumble at the arbitrary bullying of a "blue-bottle." If a Field Marshal shoot a man by mistake, you cry, "murder:" if a judge hang the wrong individual, you term it a mistake. You are furiously prejudiced on this point, and you have a right to your prejudices—you can administer your own household affairs according to any whim, called system, which obtains for a while over its fellows. But when you thrust your enlightened institutions, the growth of slowly rolling centuries, upon the semi-barbarians of the Ionian Isles, and the rugged ruffians of Affghanistan, then you pass the fine limit of things proper. Then you act like a professed philanthropist, very benevolently, and in my humble opinion, very mischievously, very unwisely

But of what use all this iteration? It has been said to you a hundred times over, and in vain. You are of a ticklish age just now, sir, like a lady on the verge of forty. You will extend the principle, amongst other wild fancies, of laying down a railroad where the neighbourhood requires a footpath; you are determined to carry out in politics, as in topical improvements, this system of end-without-beginning. If India were blessed with a military government, what is to become of the Civil Service?—what of the Briton's boast that all the world over his law is one and the same?

These puzzles I cannot solve: still, Mr. Bull, still I venture to believe that one of these days, as the nursery phrase is, India will be blessed with a military government.

And now, as you are beginning to look intensely surly, we will,—as ancient matrons say when they have succeeded in making a conversation thoroughly distasteful,—"change the subject, de-ar!"

* * * *

Some years ago, when surveying the country about this Hoosree, I had an opportunity of reading a lecture to a gentleman about your age, sir:—hear how politely he received it, without ever using the word "dogmatical," or making the slightest allusion to "forwardness."

I was superintending the shampooing* of a fighting cock—about as dunghill and "low-caste" a bird as ever used a spur, but a strong spiteful thing, a sharp riser, and a clean hitter withal. Bhujang,† the "dragon" had sent many a brother biped to the soup-pot. Ere the operation of rubbing him down ended, in walked an old Moslem gentlemen, who had called in a friendly unceremonious way to look at and chat with the stranger.

Cocking, you must know, Mr. Bull, is not amongst these people the "low" diversion your good lady has been pleased to make it. Here a man may still fight his own bird and beat his own donkey *à discrétion*, without incurring the persecutions of a Philo-beast Society.

* As Orientals generally fight their birds without spurs, they pay extraordinary attention to feeding, training, and exercising them. They are sweated and scoured with anxious care, dosed (in my poor opinion a great deal too much) with spices and drugs most precisely, and made to pass hours in running, flying, and leaping. The shampooing is intended to harden their frames; it is done regularly every day, morning and evening. A fair course of training lasts from three weeks to a month, and the birds are generally brought out in excellent condition.

† Game-cocks, like chargers, are always called by some big and terrible name.

There was a humorous twinkle in the Senior's sly eye as it fell upon the form of Bhujang, and the look gained intensity when, turning towards me, the scrutiniser salaamed and politely ejaculated,

"Mashallah—that is a bird!—the Hyderabad breed,* or the Affghan?"

I shuffled off the necessity of romancing about my dunghill's origin, and merely replied that, struck by his many beauties, I had bought him of some unknown person—I did not add for eightpence.

"What Allah pleases!—it is a miraculous animal! You must have paid his weight in silver! Two hundred rupees or three hundred?"†

Many people are apt to show impatience or irritability when being "made fools of"—whereby, methinks, they lose much fun and show more folly than they imagine. My answer to the old gentleman's remark was calculated to persuade that most impertinently polite personage that the Frank, with all his Persian and Arabic, was a "jolly green."

* The game-cocks of Hyderabad, in the Deccan, are celebrated throughout India for their excellence and rarity. So difficult is it to purchase birds of purest blood, that I have heard of a rich Moslem visiting the Nizam's capital for the purpose of buying eggs.

† The usual price of a first-rate cock is *3l.* or *4l.* My friend was indulging his facetiousness when he named *20l.* or *30l.*

Thereupon, with the utmost suavity he proceeded to inform me that he also was a fighter of cocks, and that he had some—of course immeasurably inferior to the splendid animal being shampooed there—which perhaps might satisfy even my fastidious taste. He concluded with offering to fight one under the certainty of losing it,* but anything for a little sport; again gauged me with his cunning glance, salaamed, and took his leave.

In the evening, after prayers, appeared Mr. Ahmed Khan, slowly sauntering in, accompanied by his friends and domestics: a privileged servant carrying in his arms a magnificent bird, tall, thin, gaunt, and active, with the fierce, full, clear eye, the Chashmi Murwarid,† as the Persians call it; small, short, thin, taper head, long neck, stout crooked back, round, compact body, bony, strong, and well-hung wings, stout thighs, shanks yellow as purest gold and huge splay claws—in fact, a love of a cock.

I thought of Bhujang for a moment despairingly.

After a short and ceremonious dialogue, in which the old gentleman "trotted" me out very much to his

* The usual wager is the body of the bird killed or wounded.

† The "pearl eye."

own satisfaction and the amusement of his companions, the terms of the wager were settled, and Bhujang was brought in struggling upon his bearer's bosom, kicking his stomach, stretching his neck, and crowing with an air, as if he were the *Sans-peur* of all the cocks. "There's an animal for you!" I exclaimed, as he entered. It was a rich treat to see the *'goguenard* looks of my native friends.

Countenances, however, presently changed, when sending for a few dozen Indian cockspurs* like little sabres, I lashed a pair to my bird's toes, and then politely proceeded to perform the same operations to my friend's. Ahmed Khan looked on curiously. He was too much of a sportsman, that is to say, a gentleman, to hang back, although he began to suspect that all was not so right as he could have wished it to be. His bird's natural weapon was sound, thin, and sharp as a needle, low down upon the shank, at least an inch and a quarter long, and bent at the correctest angle: mine had short, ragged, and blunt bits of

* The Indian cockspur differs essentially from ours. It is a straight bit of steel varying from two to three and a half inches in length, with a blunt flat shaft, ending in a sharp sword-like blade, the handle as it were of which is bound to the bird's fore toe, shank, and hind toe. Every cockfighter has dozens of these tools, made in every possible variety of size and angle to suit the cocks.

horn—the most inoffensive weapons imaginable. But the steel levelled all distinctions.

We took up the champions, stood a few yards apart—the usual distance—placed them on the ground, and when the "*laissez aller*" was given, let go.

For some reason, by me unexplainable, the game cock, especially in this country, when fighting with a dunghill, seldom begins the battle with the spirit and activity of his plebeian antagonist. Possibly the noble animal's blood boiling in his veins at the degrading necessity of entering the lists against an unworthy adversary confuses him for the moment. However that may be, one thing is palpable, namely, that he generally receives the first blows.

On this occasion the vulgarian Bhujang, who appeared to be utterly destitute of respect for lineage and gentle blood—nay, more, like an English snob, ineffably delighted at the prospect of "thrashing" a gentleman—began to dance, spring, and kick with such happy violence and *aplomb*, that before the minute elapsed one of his long steels was dyed with the heart's-blood of his enemy.

Politeness forbad, otherwise I could have laughed

aloud at the expression assumed by the faces present as they witnessed this especial "do." Ahmed Khan, at the imminent peril of a wound from the triumphant dunghill, whom excited cowardice now made vicious as a fiend, raised his cock from the ground, looked piteously for an instant at his glazing eye and drooping head, bowed, and handed it over to me with a sigh.

Then like the parasite of Peñaflor after dinner, I thus addressed him—

"Ahmed Khan, great is the power of Allah! Did not a gnat annihilate Namrud,* the giant king? Could Rustam, the son of Zal, stand against a pistol bullet? or Antar against an ounce of aquafortis? Have you not heard of the hikmat† of the Frank, that he is a perfect Plato in wisdom and contrivance? Another time, old gentleman, do not conclude that because our chins are smooth, we are children of asses; and if you will take my advice, abstain from pitting valuable cocks against the obscure produce of a peasant's poultry yard."

* Nimrod, represented to be a cruel tyrant, who, attempting to martyr Abraham, was slain by a mosquito—sent to eat into his brain for the general purpose of pointing many a somnific oriental moral.

† Hikmat, philosophy, science, political cunning, king-craft, &c., a favourite word for head work in Central Asia.

"Wallah!" replied my visitor, all the cunning twinkle out of his eye, "I will take your advice! your words are sharp: they are the words of wisdom. But"—here obstinacy and conventionalism obscured Ahmed Khan's brighter qualities—"your bird is a wonderful bird. Mashallah! may he win many a fight, even as he has done this one!"

* * * *

At last at Nurai, near Sudderan's column.

Surely it is a great grievance in this part of Scinde, the ever-increasing length of the standard measure. Accustomed to consider a mile a mile, one does, especially when tired or hungry, feel that the term "German mile" is a kind of insult to one's understanding. So with the Scindian cos.* Moreover, this people appears to possess either a strangely inaccurate eye for determining distance, or an unexact tongue for declaring it. If you ask a wayfarer how far the next village is, he probably replies, uthe—there, close by—which means, scarcely within cannon reach. Or it is sadda pandh—a shout's length,

* The cos in India is usually about two miles long. In Scinde it varies greatly: short in the north, in the south and south-east it becomes about double the common distance.

by which you must understand that you have nothing less than four good miles before you.

We pass the night on a plain close to the spot where the Fulailee falls into the Goonee River. This, to judge from the many miles covered with broken bricks, and the ruined foundations of large buildings, was once the site of a flourishing city, doomed, like many of its fellows, to display "the havoc of the East." As usual in Scinde, a domed tomb or two, converted into pigeon-houses, are the only melancholy survivors of former magnificence; a modern mud mosque, humbly built to accommodate the sparse population of the neighbouring villages, contrasts strongly with the idea of the "things that were." This line of country was the route of the celebrated Madad Khan,* the last Affghan invader of Scinde, a successful, but ruthless soldier, who boasted that where he found a rose-garden he left salt earth.

The *locale* is not without its interest. Sudderan's

* About the close of the last century, Madad Khan was despatched by Shah Taymur, the Affghan monarch, with an overwhelming, force, to restore Miyan Abd el Nabi the Kalhora tyrant, to a throne from which he had been driven by his military vassals, the Talpur Belochies, and their followers. The general's conduct during the expedition was shamefully cruel, and therefore successful in the highest degree.

column—it does not remind you of Trajan's or Nelson's—is the resort of Hindoo pilgrims, who flock here every year in the dark half of the month Waisakh.* At that time many of the devotees shave their heads, and the whole body, male and female, first perform pradakhshina, or circumambulation, with the right side always presented to the object circumambulated, thrice round the column, in honour of it, and then each person casts seven clods, or brickbats, at the neighbouring tomb, accompanying the action with remarks the reverse of complimentary to the memory of its tenant.

When darkness falls upon us, and we return to take our ease in our tent with closed flaps, enjoying ourselves over our fireside—a hole dug in the ground and filled with burning braise—I will recount the tale to the music of the village dogs' monotonous bayings, the bubblings of our hukkahs, and the spiteful lamentations which the jackals vent upon the subject of our pertinacious vitality.

* * * *

Before the time of the Prophet—a Hindoo date,

* Waisakh, in the luni-solar year of the Hindoos, corresponds with our April and May.

popular on account of the latitude it affords—a noble city covered this plain, and extended over the far range of limestone hills, whose bifurcation limits it. And Rajah Ram was the ruler of that city, a prince renowned, as Eastern monarchs usually are in story-books, for valour, justice, and generosity; besides which he had a fine large family, for which it appears he had to thank the law of polygamy.

It so happened, that when Sudderan, the eldest of Rajah Ram's regiment of sons, arrived at the age of puberty, his mother, the favourite wife, died, and the afflicted widower, his father, speedily filled up the void which her demise had created in his heart, by taking to his bosom one of the fairest *demoiselles* in his dominions.

All the world over, the stepmother, as an order of beings, has a bad name. They are, it is said, always in extremes, either running into over-regard for, or, what is far more common, busying themselves in embittering the hours of their husband's children during his life, and appropriating their goods and chattels after his death. In this case the lady conceived a passionate affection for the young prince, her stepson, whose noble qualities, moral and physical, were—the original relator affirms, not I, Mr. John Bull—such as almost to justify the step.

One day, as Sudderan was practising archery in the palace garden, he missed his mark, and shot an arrow into his stepdame's drawing-room. The poor young man thoughtlessly ran upstairs to recover the missile, when,—oriental ladies are *naïve* in their declarations—to his horror and astonishment, the queen began to be very bold and forward. Sudderan, briefly remarking that he considered her in the light of a mother, left the room as speedily as he was allowed to do.

Rajah Ram was out hunting during the acting of this scene. No sooner did he return than, as you, or any other man, could guess, his wife determined that her hate, if not her love—the sentiments are sisters—should be gratified, denounced Sudderan to his father, upon the false charge usual on such occasions, and insisted that his wickedness deserved the severest retribution.

Like red-hot steel, as might be expected, burned the uxorious old gentleman's wrath: nothing but blood could extinguish it. Hastily calling together a few trusty followers, he left his wife's apartment, determined, with utter disregard to the best and most hackneyed bit of advice that ever issued from old Justice's prosy lips—*audi alteram partem*—upon his son's instant destruction.

Meanwhile Sudderan, who was still amusing himself in the garden, saw his father and the slaves hurrying towards him armed, and with countenances upon which malice prepense was written in the most legible characters. When it was too late, he attempted to fly. Rage winged the old rajah's steps; already, sword in hand, he was close to his son, when the good Sudderan, to save his sire from the sin of murder, prayed to Heaven for immediate death.

At that moment the young man disappeared, and a pillar of earth started into existence upon the spot, so near Rajah Ram that he ran against it, whilst a loud and terrible voice, evidently not the produce of human lungs, declared that Heaven had listened to the prayer of the innocent.

The old king's mind was enlightened by the miracle. He returned home, with a listless air, gave certain careless directions for the decapitation of his would-be Parisina, died shortly afterwards of want of appetite and that general derangement of the digestive organs, popularly called a broken heart, and was buried in that holy tomb, to be pelted and abused by many a generation of pilgrims.

The pillar unconnected with some romance is a puzzle. It is a truncated cone of the mud used in Scindian buildings, about sixteen feet high and seventy-one in circumference round the base. It stands upon a mound of the same material, and the whole covers a natural platform of limestone rock.

Easily climbing to the top by one of the wide clefts which rain has dug in the side of the tumulus, I found a shaft sunk perpendicularly down to the foundation. Below the base was another cut, into which I penetrated despite the fiends and dragons, the cobras and scorpions with which my friends the natives peopled it; it was about seven or eight feet in length, and led nowhere. These, I afterwards heard, were the work of Ghulam Ali Talpur, one of the late princes who, suspecting, as an Oriental always does, that treasure was to be found in, under, or somewhere about the mysterious erection, took the most energetic steps to discover it, and to no purpose.

Sudderan's pillar cannot be ancient, unless, at least, it is indebted for preservation to the active hand of the devotee; the very dew would melt it away in the course of a century. Similar remains are not uncommon in this part of Scinde; they are the round towers of the country; all of them pegs for tradition, and possibly, at some future time, material for archæological discussion. On the Ganjah hills, about three miles from Sudderan's, there is another tumulus similar in all things to this, except that it is now in a very ruinous state. The people have named it after a dog, whose superior sagacity discovered the spot in which thieves had buried his owner's property. Like Sudderan's tale, the poor animal's runs in the established course of such events. He afterwards lost his life, by his master's hasty choler of course. And of course, in due time, that is to say, when too late, the master discovered his mistake, repented his conduct, and erected this monument to the memory of his Kutto.*

* A hound; the Scindians call the monument Kuttehar.

CHAPTER XIX.

A RIDE TO MEER IBRAHIM KHAN TALPUR'S VILLAGE.

Christmas day!

Without intending to string together a series of sentences which aim at the sentimental and hit the mawkish, I must draw your attention, Mr. John Bull, to what, perhaps, you are feeling without being ready to clothe the sensation in words, namely, that of all the melancholy suicidal seasons, none so bad as a birthday, an old festival, or any other time connected with the memory of the past, coming round upon the sojourner in a strange land.

To-day for instance. It is eleven o'clock. Part of you is riding in heathen garb, spear in hand, over a scorched plain, or down a sandy canal, burned by the sun upon the chills of morning, and with breakfast *in posse* not *in esse.* You jog along, as the Italian hath it, *cupo concentrato.* Suddenly you draw rein—

your eyes fix—your mind is in your ears. That joyous carolling of distant church bells, whence can it come? Whence? whence? you puzzle over the question. How wonderful it is: now full and sonorous, as if the breeze brought every pulsation of sound directly to your senses: now soft and mellowed by distance, till scarcely heard in the hum of day. You can scarcely persuade yourself that it is a false creation, proceeding from the heat-oppressed brain, that delusively speaks—the twanging of some over-excited nerve—a mere revival of things obsolete and forgotten.

The sun sets. Darkness drops upon you like a shroud, instead of delicately encircling you with the several shades and gradations of twilight. You return from your absent and disconsolate evening's stroll to your lonely ill-lit tent: you prepare for your dinner, a boiled barn-door, with a *bifteck* of goat. What visions are causing your black valet to wonder at your moodiness, while you discuss the unpalatable morsel?

Finally you retire: you turn your face towards the tent wall and — weep? No! or sleep? No! The frown of night and the silence of solitude deepen the gloom about your heart. For hours you lie awake, rolling restlessly from side to side, as if each new thought left a sting in you. You *think.* Your eyes have another sight; your ears a hearing which scarcely belongs to them; even your material nose becomes spiritually affected. In a moment you are severed from yourself—miraculously I should almost say—by such lands and such seas! You annihilate time as you do space: you are Jack, Johnny, Master John, and Mister John Bull, all in the twinkling of an eye, the scenes of by-gone days being rehearsed with a vividness which startles you. Again you hear the dear familiar voices of family and friends ringing upon the tympanum of your soul; again there are smiles and frowns for you, and words of greeting and words of rebuke. The very roast beef and plum pudding of former days appear to you with all their accidents.

Then you start up with an impatient yearning, a longing to be where you cannot be. Where you cannot be, you repeat, and yet you feel that had you wings they would be too slow for you. The truth weighs you down; you sink back, mournfully acknowledging that you are and must be where you are. At last you fall asleep; you enter the land of dreams: your mind decidedly leaves your body, and for a moment or two you enjoy your desire.

We have all heard and read of preternatural appearances of persons to persons—of shadowy forms meeting, it is believed, the eye of sense. Are these things mere delusions? Or, is there some yet unexplained law in the spiritual creation which permits Will under certain conditions to perform a feat savouring of the miraculous. Certainly, if man hath a soul, and if souls be capable of wandering forth from their cellules of flesh, we might reasonably believe that when his whole thoughts have internally deserted him and transferred themselves to other objects, the absent and the distant, his spiritual being accompanies them in the form of a "real presence."

Enough of metaphysics. At all times they are a labyrinth of words—an intricate way leading roundabouts to nowhere—a Chinese puzzle, admirably calculated unprofitably to perplex one. The moralist must be slipped at you, Mr. Bull. Anent these repinings, he will assure you solemnly that you are bound to consider what there is happy, not what there is unhappy in your lot; for instance, that on this Christmas day you are not reduced to dining on white ants, and quenching your thirst by masticating a musket bullet; that you are not "floored" by a fever, or that some tiger-like negro is not sitting perched upon your chest, sawing away at your windpipe with his long knife: and severely sententious does he become when you ironically laugh out something about gratitude and small mercies. The religionist with reverend countenance, after entering into the general history of Christmas day, will admonish you—

Naughty old man, to be so nearly asleep!

* * * *

It is time to be stirring, sir; mount your horse and turn his head towards the Goonee River in a south-east direction; and use your spurs, or we shall be well nigh famished ere we reach the village of Meer Ibrahim Khan Talpur.

In that preserve, the Haran Shikargah, as it is called, occurred to me one of those small adventures, generally comical to all but the actual actor when occurring, and comical even to him after that it has become an occurrence. A friend, Lieut. B——, and I, attended by a host of beaters, with loud lungs, long poles, and all the appurtenances of that Eastern species of the pointer or the retriever, had been passing a day of happiness in firing away round after round at the troops of wild fowl that tenant the ponds and pools. Never before did I witness such a monster meeting of bipeds feathery; they darkened the surface of the waters, and when they arose the noise of their wings was, without exaggeration, like the growling of a distant thunder-cloud. Col. Hawker himself could not have desired better sport; only he would probably have remembered a duck gun, and have knocked up for himself some kind of punt, both which desirables we neglected to provide ourselves with.

Towards the conclusion of the day, as we were preparing to beat a retreat, we came in sight of a little Jheel (lake) upon which thousands of the enemy, Chinese-like, were cackling, feeding, swimming, and otherwise disporting themselves. It was agreed, *nem. con.*, that, as a little afterpiece to the tragical work, we should settle as many of them as six or eight barrels could.

"Creep over to the other side of the Jheel," whispered my friend, "blaze into 'em sitting, and send 'em over this way—I'll drive them back to you."

"Very well, old fellow—keep the beaters here."

My path lay across a kind of ditch that connected two ponds. Thinking to wade it easily, I never thought of leaping it, and so in a surprisingly short space of time I found myself head over ears in mud and water — intimately mixed, the latter ingredient however preponderating in quantity.

Sir, with a pair of large jack-boots and wide Turkish trowsers, with a shooting-jacket composed of oil cloth, hare pockets, and a double-barrelled gun in your hand, it is, I may observe, by no means an easy matter to swim. Generally the harder you strike out, and the more vigorously you spring upward, the deeper and the more rapidly you appear to descend. Unwilling to lose my "Westley and Richards," I still kept firm hold of it, hoping with the disengaged fingers to scramble upon the side. It was like catching at a straw. The soft slimy bank, instead of affording any purchase to my clawings, yielded as if it had been butter in the dog days. Things were beginning to wear a serious look; it was impossible to shout as my mouth would not keep above water; down fell the gun totally forgotten, and a gulp or two of thick beverage was an earnest, as it were, that Kismet, after conveying me safely half round the globe had set her heart upon drowning me in a ditch. With one last frantic effort I dug my nails deep into the greasy bank, and hung on grimly as did Quasimodo's victim to the roof's edge; when suddenly with a crash and a splash I went deep under the water once more. My friend had caught sight of my predicament, and eager to save me had rushed up to the rescue. In the ardour of his anxiety, somewhat overrating his saltatory powers, he had charged the brook, fallen short in his spring, and had reluctantly taken the only means of saving himself a "ducking" similar to mine, by alighting upon my shoulders, and vigorously scrambling up the back of my head.

However we were not drowned, Mr. Bull—I take no notice of your looks. Here the adventure ended. The beaters rushed up shrieking with terror; they expected to be hung, at least, if either of us had lost our lives. I was pulled out by the collar, a mass of mud and water-bags; the gun was recovered by diving; and half-an-hour afterwards two individuals in shirts and terminations—regular Anglo-Indian and spectre huntsmen—were gazed at, shuddered at, and exorcised, by the startled peasantry as they, the riders, dashed at full gallop through the twilight in fearful anticipation of—a bad cold.

* * * *

We are now in the provinces inhabited by the Jats. Your eye is scarcely grown critical enough in this short time, to see the tweedle-dum and tweedle-dee-like difference between their personal appearance and that of the Scindians: nor can I expect you as yet to distinguish a Jat wandh (village) from a Scinde goth (village,) so I will describe them to you. You are certain to take some interest in a race which appears to be the progenitor of the old lady in a red cloak, whose hand, in return for the cunning nonsense to which her tongue gave birth, you once crossed with silver; and the wiry young light-weight, whose game and sharp hitting you have more than once condescended to admire.

Our authors* err when they suppose the Jat to be the aboriginal Hindoo of Scinde converted to Islam.

* Particularly Captain Postans. "Personal Observations on Scinde," Chapter III. I have already referred to the Jats in a former work, and hope at some future time to produce detailed ethnical reasons for identifying them with the gipsies.

Native historians and their own traditions concur in assigning to them a strange origin; their language, to this day a corrupt dialect of that spoken throughout the Indine provinces of the Punjab, gives support and real value to the otherwise doubtful testimony. It is probable that compelled to emigrate from their own lands, by one of the two main causes that bring about such movements in the East, war or famine, they travelled southward about the beginning of the eighteenth century of our era.

Under the Kalora dynasty, when Scindians composed the aristocracy as well as the commonalty of the country, the Jats, in consequence of their superior strength, their courage, and their clannish coalescence, speedily rose to high distinction. The chiefs of tribes became nobles, officials, and ministers at court; they provided for their families by obtaining grants of land—feofs incidental to certain military services—and for their followers by settling them as tenants on their wide estates. But the prosperity of the race did not last long. They fell from their high estate when the Belochies, better men than they, entered the country, and began to forage for themselves in it: by degrees, slow yet sure, they lost all claims to rank, wealth, and office. They are found scattered throughout Scinde, generally preferring the south-eastern provinces, where they earn a scanty subsistence by agriculture, or they roam over the barren plains feeding their flocks upon the several oases; or they occupy themselves in breeding, tending, training, and physicking the camel. With the latter craft their name has become identified — a Jat and a sarwan* being synonymous in Scindian ears.

The Jats in appearance are a swarthy and uncomely race, dirty in the extreme; long, gaunt, bony, and rarely, if ever, in good condition. Their beards are thin, and there is a curious expression in their eyes. They dress like Scindians, preferring blue to white clothes, but they are taller, larger, and more un-Indian in appearance. Some few, but very few, of their women are, in early youth, remarkable for soft and regular features; this charm, however, soon yields to the complicated uglinesses brought on by exposure to the sun, scanty living, and the labour of baggage cattle. In Scinde the Jats of both sexes are possessed of the virtues especially belonging to the oppressed

* A camel-man.

and inoffensive Eastern cultivator; they are necessarily frugal and laborious, peaceful, and remarkable for morality in the limited sense of aversion to intrigue with members of a strange kaum.* I say, in Scinde; this is by no means the reputation of the race in the other parts of Central Asia, where they have extended. The term "Jat," is popularly applied to a low and servile creature, or to an impudent villain; and in spite of the Tohfat el Kiram,† a Beloch would consider himself mortally affronted were you to confound his origin with the caste his ancestors deposed, and which he despises for having allowed itself to be degraded. The Brahuis, Affghans, and Persians, all have a bad word to say of them.

* * * *

Fourteen or fifteen miles from Sudderan's column to Ibrahim Khan's village. At this time of the year sand-storms begin about 10 o'clock. One's only chance of escaping them is to rise early in spite of the dry, searching, uncomfortable cold, and to reach the halting-place before their hour.

The country hereabouts, you see, is irrigated by a

* In the language of the Jat, a "kaum" is a clan.

† The author of this well known Persian History of Scinde, asserts that the Jats and the Belochies are both sprung from the same ancestors.

number of water-courses, large and small, derived from the large branches filled with water by the main trunk during the inundation. What affects one with surprise at once in the disposition of these works is their great and useless number. In some places, three deep trenches, perhaps twenty feet broad, run parallel with and close by one another, for miles and miles through the land. You will not be astonished by the peculiarity when you hear the obvious reasons for it. Each canal when excavated belonged to some native chief, whose estate lay upon the bank; and an attempt to borrow water without leave in these regions, would have excited a storm of wrath violent as that would be in your bosom, Mr. Bull, were a stranger to lay his hand upon your cotton. So where we are now riding, for instance, the northern channel belonged to a Chandiyo Beloch, the southern one to a Changiyo, whilst the central bed conveyed water to private property and government lands lying beyond reach of the other two.

You may also remark, that the heads of these canals are usually so placed that the drift of sand carried down the main stream may choke them up as soon as possible. The rise and fall of ground was calculated by the practised eye—spirit-levels being things unknown—consequently the line of direction was, in one case out of ten, chosen for the best. The banks instead of being disposed at a convenient angle, were made either perpendicular or to lean the wrong way, so as to be undermined by the current, and to occasion as much labour and loss of time to the excavators as even the latter, gainers by the thing, could desire. The prodigious tortuousness of the bed may appear to you the result of calculation, an attempt to make natural locks: quite the contrary; it is the effect of ignorance, these abrupt windings being intended to get over the difficulty of some trifling rise.

This is the dead season in Scinde. The fields, small and rare amongst the luxuriant masses of nature's plantations, in form of jao, karel, and jhill,* are covered over with a stratum of white, shiny clay, with isolated stubbles projecting from it, like the stray hairs on a very old gentleman's unperuked pate. The water when it remains in the river beds

* Various wood-like shrubs, which being interpreted by hard Latin words, become about as unintelligible after translation as before.

below the banks is even more offensive than that of Father Thames; the trees are withered and scraggy; the straggling villages are surrounded by heaps of dried-up thorn. Nothing but the sunshine seems to flourish—nothing to abound but dust and glare.

The labourers, or rather the lucky part of the labouring population, are at work—if that English phrase be allowed—on the canals. In winter they will do anything to save themselves from semi-starvation. Yet observe their characteristic apathy. The head man, who receives from Government 2*l.* per man, in consideration of his gang of 150 men, lies dozing drunk under a sheet stretched between two giant thorn bushes. Although the work is done by contract, and for every rupee a cubit in depth, by one in breadth, and eighteen in length, must be excavated, at least half the diggers are squatting torpidly on their hams, looking at the different pits, which at this stage of their labours are dug in the clayey deposit of the inundation. Those that are not sitting or standing lazily scrape up the cake with dwarf hoes, and, *à plusieurs reprises,* transfer it to shallow baskets of wicker-work, little bigger than soup plates, with which they load their heads. Then groaning under the weight of five pounds, they slowly toil up the steps cut out in the precipitous side of the canal, and throw down their burden, to save trouble, upon its edge, thereby annually adding a few cubic feet to the spoil banks that encumber it. Such toil requiring refection, they sit down for a minute or two under the mimosas that spring where mulberries ought to grow, gazing listlessly upon the scene and the society of their toils; then rising again with the usual half-grunt, half-groan, they crawl down the steps, slowly and unwillingly, as schoolboys wending their way to the "seminary." The favourite occupation below is to stand by the bars, or bench-marks left in the bed of the canal for convenience of measuring work done, and to shape the short parapets of silt into mathematically accurate right angles. Every half hour all smoke, and at a certain time each man applies himself to the bhang, of which he has been dreaming all the morning. This is the way during the cold season. As the year advances, the "navvies" will refuse to work between the hours of 11 and 3, because labouring in the heat of the sun does not suit the fragility of their constitutions; and when the inundation approaches they will run away, if not allowed to depart in peace, for the purpose of preparing their fields.

A European officer, it is true, superintends each district. But he has, probably, 300 canals to look after, and by the condition of his nature he cannot be ubiquitous. The evil result of the natives' indolence is, that a bed thirty feet broad will, in the course of a few years contract to half its original dimensions, till at last a deep cunette measurable by inches is all that remains of the canal, the rest of it becoming a footpath for travellers human and bestial. The tail of the channel, of course, shrinks miserably in length, because the trunk has not been sufficiently excavated, probably an inch having been gained upon every mile of sole. When there is water in the bed some noble feoffee will take the liberty of throwing embankments across it, so as to monopolise the produce of it for his Persian wheels. By abundant activity and attention, the European overseer will sometimes discover a flagrant abuse; such as a canal reported cleared out, but never touched: at the same time, the amount of undiscovered rascality, small, but by degrees becoming uncomfortably great, is amply sufficient to hinder the improvement of the country.

Scinde, Mr. John Bull, is an Eastern Ireland on a large scale. The idle fools, her male children, will not work; they would almost rather starve: the women and infants declare they cannot work; all would rather want with ease than be wealthy with toil. Were you to relieve their necessities, Hibernian like, they would but curse the niggard hand that only feeds and clothes them. The only chance of reclaiming the country, is to provide the people with peculiar facilities for emigration, or to leaven the dull mass by an infusion of the manly races that tenant the neighbouring mountains. The latter experiment might easily and profitably be tried. Every year we could induce thousands of Brahuis and Belochies from the Kelat Hills to spend the cold season on the plains, with the express proviso of being allowed to return for the summer to their families and homes, for the eight or ten shillings a month which an able-bodied man may earn at this work. A single little Highlander would do the work of three Scindians.

* * * *

We are approaching the village, our halting place, as sundry signs and symptoms show. An unfortunate tracksman meets us, and—these people are powerful at hoping—warmed by the sight of our unusual coloured countenances, outs with a long dole concerning a lost camel, whose foot-prints he swears by all the saints in his calendar, lead directly to Ibrahim Khan's gate. The cultivators stand at the doors of their huts, howling that they have not had a drop of water over their fields for the last two years, and the Hindoo banyans, quitting their shops to catch hold of our stirrups, offer us all the blessings of Heaven if we will only induce their lord to pay his lawful debts. For this case I have very little pity; it is rascal *versus* rascal. When we left Hyderabad, the price of wheaten flour was one shilling for 16 lb. Here we can only get 10 lb. for the money, and our servants who require at least a seer * a day, find it difficult to exist upon their eight or ten rupees per mensem. I rather envy Ibrahim Khan's facilities for fleecing these withholders of corn from the poor. The traders are now all occupied in buying and plastering up grain,† causing a factitious famine in order to raise the value of the article as the inundation approaches, and the

* About two pounds.

† It is stored hereabouts in large conical heaps, covered over with a thick coating of kahgil.

material for sowing is required by the peasant. The poor tracksman and the ryots we must publicly scold for daring to appeal to us, and privately commiserate.

A sawari, or retinue, comes forth to meet and greet the "distinguished strangers." The leader, our host's nephew, a lean, ill-visaged, beetle-browed, thin-lipped Beloch, habited in a cap of green and gold cloth; a long, quilted, gaudy-coloured, chintz coat and blood-red sutthan,* apologises at uncomfortable length, with the usual toilsome politeness, for his uncle's "apparent rudeness" in not being "present in our service"—the sardar, or head of the house, I gather from his hints, is engaged in his favourite pastime, hawking. More will be said of this event anon. At present you may remark that a native *cortège* is anything but a pleasant thing. Our friends are mounted on fat, fidgetty, high-fed Nizamani mares, who wince and prance, curvet and dance, like so many Florence hacks, when they meet a party of ladies. The pace, a confused amble, half-trot half-canter, though good in its proper place, is quite the reverse of agreeable in these processions; if the

* The wide drawers tight round the ancle.

weather be cold, you freeze for want of exercise; if hot, you pant and fret yourself and your horse into a foam from the over-abundance of it. Every now and then, as our fellows exchange the friendliest greetings with perfect strangers, and almost throw themselves from their saddles to shake frequent hands, a neigh—a scream—a whisking of the tail—a kick, succeeded by a shower of the same kind, occur to vary the excitements of the scene. It is useless to beg for a little room, or to glance helplessly at our legs; honour is done to us by crowding around us—the more we decline it, the more sedulously it is thrust upon us. The only chance of escaping it is to explain that we Franks, as a nation, never ride at any pace but full gallop. We may thus get rid of our troublesome friends; most of them will be run away with by their restiff nags, and the rest will be left far behind, drumming, with vicious but harmless heels, the sides of their ragged galloways.

There is the village—if village it be—a collection of huts and gardens clustering round a tolerable-sized house, the *facsimile*, in outward semblance, of our quondam royal abode at Hyderabad. Our *cortège*, I gathered, was expecting that we should at once enter the "palace," where, in all probability we should find the sardar, who is out hawking, sitting in state to receive us; we must do no such thing; to-morrow will convince you that a Scinde visit is too soporific an affair to be ushered in by a long weary ride. Besides, as the khan did not put himself out to come and meet us, we shall display useful "dignity" by not evincing too much anxiety or hurry to meet him. This *à part* of the greater consideration that he would insist upon our becoming his guests; whereas our tents, pitched under a clump of sweet evergreens, will be far more comfortable than a flea-ridden Scindian *palazzo*. We have also a little travelling business to transact at this our first halt. The camel courier, who fetches our papers and pickles, hams and beer, from Hyderabad, has levanted, beast, cargo, and all—a fact which calls loudly for a report to the police-office. Our nags are footsore with the heat of the sand, and more than half blinded by the glare of the sun—we must blister their eyes with garlic,* and cold-water-bandage their legs.

Also, before we meet the Talpur chief, Meer

* This operation is generally performed by drawing a circle of garlic juice or the milk of the fire plant round the eye. It is a desperate remedy, as it marks the skin indelibly.

Ibrahim Khan, we must elicit from our moonshee all the *scan. mag.* current about him and his family; number congees, weigh out compliments, and measure the distance we must advance towards the door.

CHAPTER XX.

MEER IBRAHIM KHAN TALPUR.

WHILST I am conversing with the moonshee, Mr. John Bull, it might be as well if you would take up a book and be engrossed with its contents: there is nothing that a native dislikes more than the open eye, unless it be the attentive ear of a witness.

Enter Mr. Hari Chand, a portly pulpy Hindoo, the very type of his unamiable race, with a cat-like gait, a bow of exquisite finish; a habit of sweetly smiling under every emotion, whether the produce of a bribe or a kick; a softly murmuring voice, with a tendency to sinking; and a glance which seldom meets yours, and when it does, seems not quite to enjoy the meeting. How timidly he appears at the door! How deferentially he slides in, salaams, looks deprecating, and at last is induced to sit down! Above all things how he listens! Might he not be mistaken for a novel kind of automaton, into which you can transfer your mind and thoughts — a curious piece of human mechanism in the shape of a creature endowed with all things but a self.

You would start could you read his thoughts at the very moment that you are forming such opinions of him.

"Well, Hari Chand (after the usual salutations), and pray what manner of man may be this Meer Ibrahim Khan,—Talpur, is he not?"

"Wah! wah!! What a chieftain! — what a very Nushirawan* for all-shading equity!—a Hatim for overflowing generosity,—a Rustam—"

"That is to say, always considering that he is a Beloch,"—says Hari Chand, perceiving by the expression of my face that his opinion requires modifying.—

"For a Beloch! The Sahib's exalted intelligence has of course comprehended the exact fact, that they are all dolts, asses, fools. But this Ibrahim Khan, saving the Sahib's presence, is not one of *them*. —Quite the contrary."—

"You mean he is a rogue!"

* The just king of Persia.

"The Sahib has the penetration of an arrow—a rogue of the first water!"—

Remark, Mr. Bull, that the native of India, and the adjacent parts of Central Asia, parcels out his brethren into two great bodies—knaves and fools; and what is wiser still, he acts upon the conviction that they are such. The division, you must own, is remarkable for a pregnant simplicity, and eminent adaptation for practical purposes. With that little talisman ever hanging round his neck, to be consulted on all occasions where he has dealings with another, the Oriental manages to get through life as if he carried an old woman's blessing upon his head, or a decoy dollar in his hand. Of course, in hot youth, he makes his mistakes. Sometimes he is deceived by the foolish look of a knave, or the knavish look of a fool. Occasionally he is puzzled by one of the cross-breeds, to which the blending of the psychologic extremes hath given birth. But he begins early in life the business of life; he works at it with admirable singleness of purpose, and by that malignant labour which conquers all things he seldom fails to become master of the subject, as far as it goes, long before one hair of his beard turns grey.

—"A rogue of the first water. He has won the wealth of Bokhara and Samarcand by the sunshine of the countenance of the Honourable Company, to whom he sells camels at six pounds a-head, after compelling his subjects to receive two pounds for them. Ah! well said the poet—

> "'I would rather be a companion of devils,
> Than the ryot of an unjust king.'

"He has almost doubled the size and resources of his jagir (feof), by the friendship of certain Sahibs who (here we must stop Hari Chand's tongue with a look);—and when the Valiant Company allows him twenty-thousand rupees to excavate his canals and improve his land, he—the Lord bless him!—expends half, and lays by the other moiety in his coffers."

"But," pursues Hari Chand, delighted that we allow him a reasonably free use of his subject,—"has not the Sahib seen with his own eyes what a prodigious thief he is? Did not the poor Scindian complain yesterday that his camel had been stolen from him? and the peasants that they were starving? and the Hindoos that they were ruined? Every man to be sure may cut off his own dog's tail!

It were well, however, if nothing worse could be said about this Ibrahim."

Now Mr. Hari Chand's countenance assumes that deep mysterious expression which courts the operation of "pumping." After which, chuckling internally at having secured for himself the acute gratification of being able to tear a man's reputation to shreds, he resumes in a low soft tone of voice, as if the tent walls had ears—

"He murdered his elder brother! Yes, Sahib, before the battle of Meeanee, Ibrahim was a poor sorry fellow, a cadet who was not even allowed to sit in the presence of the great. But

> 'The world is a water-wheel, and men the pots upon it,
> Now their heads are beneath the stones, now they are raised
> high to heaven.' "

—The "scorpion," Mr. Bull, as your London dowagers used to call the pauper members of a rich family, flourishes in the East as in England. In the West, probably by reason of the frigid climate and the artificial existence the animal leads, his sting though sometimes troublesome, is rarely dangerous. Here it is often fatal.—

"At the battle of Meeanee a matchlock ball pierced

the occiput of Ibrahim's elder brother, and the clan when they saw their chief bite the dust, ran away like sheep, headed by Ibrahim Khan the leader of the flock, who ran a little faster than the rest to show the line of direction. When the Fort of Hyderabad surrendered, one of the first persons that gave up his dangerous sword to the General Sahib, was Ibrahim Khan, who had the address to oust his nephew from the inheritance, and by plentiful fox-play took all the carcase from the tiger.

"And now," continues Hari Chand, anxious to improve each fleeting minute, "Ibrahim, who five years ago was not allowed to show his mouth at court, sits on a chair before the collector and pays visits to the Madams—the ladies of the English. He has ventured to boast that one of them is desperately enamoured of him (this, says Hari Chand, to himself, will irritate the fools—ourselves, Mr. Bull—beyond measure). He drinks curaçoa and brandy like a sahib. He has become proud. Yesterday, for instance, instead of coming out for miles and miles to meet the sawari."—

I knew we should end here. Envy, hatred, and malice are the seeds which the Oriental loves to scatter about as he passes over life's path—not for sheer diabolicality, but with the instinct of cunning weakness. "When thieves fall out, honest men slip in," says our trite proverb. When two thieves contend over a bone, a third finds an opportunity of carrying it off, thinks the Eastern philosopher. Now observe how carefully Hari Chand applies the lucifer to a certain fuel which he supposes every heart to contain :—

"The Sahib is a servant of the Honourable Company—long be its prosperity! Whose dog is Ibrahimoo,* that he should dare to treat the "lords of the sword and pen" † in this disgraceful way? that he should send that owl‡ of a nephew to greet them with his hootings, and venture to be absent when they arrived at his grave.§ Had Smith Sahib the collector (now I have that red-coated infidel on the hip, thinks Hari Chand) been coming with his writers, and his scribes, and his secretaries, and his guards, and all his retinue, Ibrahim would have been present to kiss his feet. And why? Because Smith Sahib

* A diminutive and decidedly disrespectful form of the proper name.

† A high title in Persia, terribly prostituted in Scinde and India.

‡ The bird of wisdom in Europe, in Asia becomes the symbol of stupidity : *vice versâ*, the European goose is the Asiatic emblem of sageness.

§ A metaphor, by no means complimentary, for his house and home.

is a —— good easy man, who allows the bandit to do what he pleases. Ah, well said Nizami,*

'The joys of this world!—donkeys have engrossed them,
Would to Allah, Nizami had been a donkey!'

"But, perhaps," continues Hari Chand during a short pause, in which time his mind had been almost preternaturally active, "it is not so much Ibrahim's crime as that of Kakoo Mall."

"And who may Kakoo Mall be?"

"Kakoo Mall? The Sahib does not know who Kakoo Mall is? Ibrahim's head moonshee, a Khudabadi Banyan of a fellow, (our man, Mr. Bull, is a Sehwani, a Green instead of a Brown) and one of the most unscrupulous ruffians that ever carried inkstand in his belt."

Thereupon a fierce worrying of Kakoo Mall's character. In common charity I would draw our man off, only that most probably Kakoo Mall is about this time abusing us and Hari Chand to Ibrahim Khan, just as violently as Hari Chand abuses Ibrahim and Kakoo Mall to us.

He will, I would swear, do his best that your

* A first-rate Persian poet infinitely celebrated and popular for satire, morality, and gross indecency.

honours may not be treated with the courtesy due to your rank, and that I, your servant, may be insulted."

"Very well, moonshee, we will look after him. You may go. At eleven we start for our visit. Be ready to accompany us; and don't be afraid of Kakoo Mall."

"Under the shadow of your eagle wings," replies Hari Chand, with a lovely bow, "what have I to fear from the puny talons of the carrion crow?"

* * * *

We mount our horses, still in native costume, and cross the village, our moonshee ambling by our side, and a few ferocious Affghan servants bringing up the rear, much to the astonishment and quite to the admiration of its inhabitants.

We reach the court-yard gate of the Talpur's dwelling. Three ragged rascals, with sheathed swords in their hands and daggers in their belts, headed by another nephew, rush up to us as if their intention were to begin by cutting our throats. The young chief, seizing our hands, chatters forth a thousand congratulations, salutations and messages, nearly tears us from our saddles, and demands concerning our happiness, in tones which rise high above the whooping and yelling of his followers. One fellow rushes away to pass the word " they come." And out pours a whole rout to witness the event, and, by their presence, to communicate to it all possible importance.

After jostling and being jostled through half-a-dozen narrow gateways, we arrive opposite the verandah, under which stands Meer Ibrahim Khan Talpur. I see this reception is to be a poor attempt at court ceremonial.

We dismount—twenty men pressing forward to hold our stirrups—the whole party yelling " Bismillah," (in the name of Allah !) as our feet touch the ground. Then Ibrahim Khan, pressing forward—seizes our hands—wrings our arms in their sockets, and—oh compliment with which we might readily have dispensed!—precipitates himself upon our bosoms, clasping us firmly to a " corporation," and applying a rough-bearded chin to the upper portions of both our shoulder-blades consecutively.

We are led in with our slippers on. Our host has not removed his, consequently we will continue to wear ours. Another volley of inquiries, and another series of huggings, as we are led up to the silken ottoman, upon which he, the chief, and his eldest nephew are to sit—a motley crowd of relations, friends, acquaintances, dependants, and any one who happened to be passing the house at the time, pressing in, looking curiously at us and fearfully at our retainers. All arrange themselves with the noise of a troop of ravens upon the floor.

Observe, Mr. John Bull, in the corner of the room Hari Chand and Kakoo Mall, almost weeping with joy, throw themselves upon each other, and murmur *mezzo voce* thanks to that Heaven which hath thus permitted the tree of Hope to put forth green leaves and to bear sweet fruit.

Charming this choice blossom of true civilization blooming amid the desert of barbarism around it! Had a violet or a forget-me-not appeared to us in the centre of Ibrahim Khan's court-yard, the sight would scarcely have been more suggestive. What memories it revives!—one of them—

When the fascinating Lady F. Macarthy, an authoress and a *femme d'esprit*, had sketched with a pencil, stolen from Wit, the character of her bosom friend, Miss Anne Clotworthy Crawley, and published the same, the English world laughed, but Dublin joyed with double joy.

Dublin joyed thus, firstly at seeing the picture, secondly at foreseeing the scene it would occasion when the sketcher and the sketched met for the first time in public. There was much of anticipation, much of vague and happy expectation in this idea.

Was it disappointed?

No. At the next ball, Lady Florence, unwilling to show Miss Crawley that she could not use as well as abuse a friend, and Miss Crawley, as unwilling to show Lady Florence her consciousness of having been abused as she deserved; both with one impulse at the same moment clave the crowd, and—they had been parted at least five days—kissed each other with all the ardour of feminine friendship.

"And 'faith"—said every Irishman of the hundred who witnessed the scene—"and 'faith, I' disp'hised them both!"

Kiss on, Kakoo Mall and Hari Chand!

* * * *

Now for a survey of our host and the state apartment in which he has been pleased to receive us.

Instead of bare stuccoed walls, a floor but partially carpeted with a Persian rug or two, and a single settee at the upper part of the room, here we have an Oriental imitation of an English saloon: tables, chairs, framed prints, doors and glass windows, forming salient points of resemblance. As usual, there is an intense grotesqueness in the general appearance. Liqueur bottles and a large pipe lie upon rosewood dressing-cases, appropriated to display, a French clock, with its erect Bayard, stands in silent majesty upon a shelf cut out in the wall; several landscapes are hung upside down, a therm-antidote is placed in a corner carefully beyond reach of the wind; a lady's glove, treasured as a great curiosity, peeps from the folds of another great curiosity, a pair of "leathers;" and a noble goshawk perches upon the back of a well-wadded, crimson-velvetted *bergère*, et cetera.

Had we called early in the morning, we might have found our noble entertainer sitting in a coloured cotton waistcloth, *pour toute toilette*, his hair plastered over with clay, and his palms full of kussumba.*

* Kussumba in Scinde, is the name given in good society to the infusion of opium, which the natives extensively use.

Now, however, he is in grand costume; a cylindrical cap of gold brocade covering his curly black locks, gathered into a knot upon the poll of his head, and flattened out upon his temples, as if the "bands" had been ironed: beautifully accurate is his beard, and of his moustaches not one hair passes another, or wanders from its proper place. His vest is of the crimsonest satin, richly embroidered with startling silks in intricate patterns; around his waist a fine Tattah shawl supports his ivory-hilted poniard: a pair of loose trousers, azure blue, the favourite Beloch colour, falling over yellow cordovan slippers, conclude a costume which, with the exception of the cap and the "gingerbread work" on the coat, is at once manly and magnificent. He has no gems about him except the large emerald which glitters upon the hilt of his "dangerous sword," and no ornament but a gold hoop with a silver slab on his fore finger —a signet ring intended for use, not for show. He will inform you, if you ask him, that he does not write himself, but that he keeps many a moonshee who is celebrated for calligraphy. Ibrahim Pacha in London, Mr. Bull, was loath to confess that he could not scrawl his name in the royal album:

Ibrahim Khan in Scinde manifestly takes pride in parading his ignorance of the unchivalrous art.

Remark his portliness, or rather obesity of person. In this, as well as in other parts of the East, beauty, male and female, goes by hundred-weights. Nasir Khan, the late ruler of Hyderabad, was considered one of the handsomest men in the country, chiefly because he could scarcely walk, and had great trouble in finding a horse to carry him. When doomed to a foreign jail, he was succeeded in part of his functions by a gentleman who rather resembled him in person; and the public of Scinde remarked with gratefulness that their favourite prince was but half lost to them, since the Company had sent them a ruler so worthy, for fatness, to succeed him. Thinness, you must know, is considered not only a personal defect, but also a sign of poverty; and the Scinde jackal, like the British Lion, instinctively snarls at the appearance of one who wants. The natives of India are like dogs in this particular: feed them, and invariably you fatten them. "Haven't you enough to eat, that you are so lean?" is the natural question put to an ensign who in these warm regions outgrows his strength. You now see the reason of my adopting the Arab costume. Arabs are allowed on sufferance to be thin without being thought hungry. At the same time, Mr. Bull, the vision finds no favour in the sight of the people. If there are any conquests to be made, you need not dread the rivalry of your companion. All the little world here will feel persuaded that the thin man who rides with the stout, silent old gentleman must be a European moonshee, or at best a small relation.

"Hor! hor!! hor!!!"—How pleasant these loud, plethoric, healthy laughs, after the villainous sounding cachinnations in which the Indian family indulges. Our fat host's jolly face—judging by it you would swear that he is the warmest-hearted fellow in the world—beams with broad smiles; and at the end of every sentence, no matter the subject, he puts in a hearty hor! hor!! What irresistibly tickles his fancy is our oriental dress: he has told me twenty times already, that it becomes us beautifully, and wonders lustily why all Franks do not throw away their scare-crow habiliments as we have done.

"Will you drink opium, since you look so like us? —hor! hor!" cries the host, with a voice which can do nothing but shout—the normal Scinde organ, and infinitely amused by the facetiousness of his own question.

I will accept, Mr. Bull, and save you from what would be an infliction, by the ready excuse that you, being a man of peculiar piety and strictness of conversation, allow no intoxicating preparations to pass your lips—in public. Our host thinks, like a *commissaire de police,* that there must be a screw loose in an Englishman *qui ne se grise pas.* However, the Scindian has delicacy enough to ponder and wonder in the depths of his own head—the Frenchman, probably, would not be so nice.

The opium—country grown, and by no means a despicable article of commerce, sir—is brought in by the head servant of the pipes, who places it before us with a wine-glass, and a lota, or pipkin, full of coldish water. Ibrahim Khan, as master of the house, dispenses it, after cutting up the mass into little square bits, about the weight of a large pill: he will take at least four of these to himself. I, not being so habituated an afimi,* content myself with one. By the good aid of our forefingers, we dissolve

* "Afim," opium; "afimi," an opium-eater.

our portions in the pot, which holds exactly enough fluid for a dose. We then strain it through any cloth that comes to hand, in order to get rid of the foreign matter—some of it none the cleanest—which it contains; then each man, holding his full wine-glass, says something polite to somebody, and swallows its contents with an air jocular from fashion, not for a reason. The "old hands" may be known by the lover-like looks which they bestow upon the sherry-coloured draught. A few mouthfuls of sweetmeat, or bits of sugar-candy, are next eaten, to bring out the effects of the drug, and the pipes are pensively smoked to while away the tedious interval.

Opium in Scinde is never inhaled, and rarely eaten. Drunk, as you have seen it, the drug is a favourite one with the rich and the great, or rather with all who have money to spend upon it. It is the best stimulant these countries afford. Many an exaggerated tale about its terrible consequences has, I know, been poured into your ears, Mr. Bull. Probably the Chinese, who, in horror of losing too much bullion, systematically denigrated the object of the foreign traffic, can claim the honour of having planted the prejudice in your stubborn mind. Of late years, men who have passed their lives in opium-eating lands, as Guzerat and Malwa, have raised their voices, striving to modify the romantic exaggeration of your opinions upon this subject. They own that to some constitutions it is a poison; moreover, that it is impossible to predict from its effect upon one person how it will affect another. They admit the truth contained in the latter half of an oft-quoted Arabic proverb—"Afim is the healer of all ills, and itself of all diseases the evilest"—meaning that the drug is a dangerous one, because the dose requires to be increased. But at the same time they assert that this may be said, with equal truth, of almost all stimulants, and that opium taken in moderation is not a whit more injurious to a man than alcohols and brandied wines. But with the "Confessions," as a warning, and Coleridge as an example—neither of them by-the-by cases in point—when will you listen to me?

Opium even when taken in large, but not increasing, quantities, seems to act beneficially upon some constitutions. I recollect an old Persian moonshee, who used regularly every day to swallow three boluses, and yet I never saw in the East a more hale or hearty old gentleman of sixty than he. There is a popular idea in Scinde, as in other oriental countries, that opium is a "brave drink." It certainly quiets the irritable nerves, and produces a peculiar stubbornness of purpose and sullenness of temper—moods invaluable to the Eastern soldier, whose battles are a succession of single combats. Bhang, on the contrary, for reasons already detailed, is the poet's, the philosopher's, and the mystic's favourite.

Such are the reflections which naturally occur during the silent quarter of an hour devoted by our society to smoking themselves "screwed." At the end of the time the host motions away his pipe, and prepares himself to converse and hor! hor! with renewed vigour.

"Were you at Nasir Khan's fight?"—so the battle of Meeanee is called by the Scindians, as opposed to Sher Mohammed's fight, the battle of Dubbah.

We reply in the negative, and suspect that we are in for one of our noble host's stock stories.

"Hor! hor! that was an affair. O Allah! Allah Akbar! was ever the like of it before?"

"Then you were present, Meer Sahib?"*

"I—yes, indeed I was. I went out with all the vassals of my poor brother (a broad grin), whom you killed. Look at his son, my nephew, there (pointing to the lean scowler sitting by his side). Well, you killed his poor father. And hor! hor! you would have killed me," pursues Ibrahim, highly amused by the idea, "but I was a little too sharp even for the Frank."

We stimulate him by an inquiry.

"How?" he vociferates, "why, when we went out of the tent to attack you, we started to hunt the deer. Some carried swords, others spears, and many sticks, because we wanted to thrash you soundly for your impudence—not to kill you, poor things. My brother—now, Allah illumine his grave!—was a simple-minded man, who said, 'What can the iron of the Angreez† do against the steel of the Beloch?'

"We drew up in a heap, eager for the onslaught. Presently some guns of yours appeared; they unlimbered; they began to fire. So did ours; but somehow or other we shot over you, you shot into us.

* The polite address to one of the blood royal.

† An allusion to the boasted superiority of what is called Damascus steel over our Sheffield cutlery.

I was on the other part of the field, so of course I didn't care much for that. But, a few minutes afterwards, what did we see?—a long red line, with flashing spikes, come sweeping over the plain towards us, like a simoom.

"Allah, Allah, what are these dogs doing? They are not running away?—All my poor brothers' men put the same question.

"Then *bang* went the great guns; *phit* the little guns; the Franks prayed aloud to the Shaitan, with a loud, horrible voice—we, to Allah. What a mosque full of mullahs it was to be sure!* Who could fight? We howled defiance against them. Still they came on. We stood and looked at them. Still they came on. We rushed and slashed at them, like Rustams. Still they came on, the White fiends.† And, by Allah, when we ran away, still they came after us. It was useless to encounter this kind of magic; the head magician sitting all the time on the back of a little bay horse, waving his hat in circles, and using words which those that

* As we should say, "What a bear garden!" Two mullahs in one mosque are sure to fight.

† One of Rustam's great exploits was slaughtering the Divi Sapid or white Demon—a personage, say the Persians, clearly typical of the modern Russians.

heard them said sounded like the language of devils. I waited till my poor brother fell dead. Then I cried to the vassals—'Ye base-born, will you see your chieftain perish unavenged?' and, having done my best to fight like a soldier, I thought I had a right to run like one—hor! hor!——

"But now tell me—you are Englishman, is there any chance of the Ameers ever returning from captivity?"

This, Mr. Bull, is our host's great bugbear—the fear lest his kinsmen should come to their own again. In truth, it is an intelligible subject of apprehension; Ibrahim Khan's head and shoulders would assuredly part company the day after our departure. The disastrous consequences of siding with the British in Affghanistan—tortures and death awaited the traitors who, after we left, remained in their native country, and all the miseries of exile, poverty, and neglect, pressed heavily upon those that followed our steps—have, I fear, done much to disperse throughout India a most pernicious suspicion that the English are not staunch friends; that they will use a man when they want him, and are then ready to cast him off, heedless as to what becomes of him. Ibrahim Khan cannot conceal his fear of such fate being in store for him. Double-dyed murderer though he may be, I do hope, for the sake of our "name," that he will escape the revengeful sabres of his kinsmen.

The assembly, after being convulsed with laughter during the chief's account of his prowess at the battle of Meeanee—there are "toadies" in Scinde as elsewhere,—was breathless, whilst he awaited our answer to his question.

"No, Meer Sahib, there is none. The morning of prosperity has at length dawned upon Scinde. It lead to a day that knows no return of night!"

"Allah Tuhar—the Lord be thy preserver!" There was no laugh as Ibrahim Khan uttered this short prayer.

* * * *

And now, having "produced an impression," we will prudently withdraw before the opium takes its full effect. I see a little horseplay commencing in different parts of the room, and our fat friend's pleasantries are beginning to verge upon the boisterous. Besides our leaving at this moment will produce a beneficial result. Ibrahim Khan has quietly but decidedly assumed the very, very great man. He expects that we should, according to custom, await his signal for ending the visit. Therefore we will do nothing of the kind, and he will respect us much the more.

"Meer Ibrahim Khan Talpur will be happy to have the company of Mr. John Bull and his companion at dinner to-day about four o'clock."—

You must not confound this *gentilezza* with one of your western invitations. Our host intends to dine at our tents, only he will send the number of fat pillaws, hot kababs, messy curries, greasy dishes of vegetables, and cakes of unleavened bread, which he himself intends to consume. We will not refuse, as the scene may be a novel one to you—a Beloch dinner party.

We rise; so does every man in the room. Vehemently are we pressed to stay. Vehemently do we refuse. Then there is a rushing to the doors, a whooping for horses, an appearance of the animals, madly kicking and plunging, because ten hands are holding each bridle, the chief accompanies us as far as the main gate of his palace, shaking hands, laughing violently, and catechising us about our healths and brains; he repeats his delight at having made friendship with us; and, as a conclusion, again clasps us to that development which would not disgrace the fat fame of a Falstaff.

I wish, Mr. John Bull, that you would not look so sheepish when being kissed. Positively you blushed this time as deeply as your boy Billy could have done—can you not, O stiff-necked old gentleman, accommodate yourself a little more readily to these habits and customs of "foreign parts?"

CHAPTER XXI.

A BELOCH DINNER AND TEA PARTY.

"A TEA-PARTY."—What horrible goblins of the past are conjured up by these three syllables!

*   *   *   *

The first object that meets our glance, as we near the tents, is a line of Belochies drawn up behind a row of earthen pots, in shape and hue by no means unlike monstrous turnips. These, the turnips, are a present of choice confectionery—material, coarse sugar, rice, flour, spices and clarified butter—always sent in token of friendship or favour. There are *ten* pots full for you, the "great gentleman," *eight* for me, the thinner man, one for our moonshee, who looks a profound disgust at not having received two, and the rest for the servants. The latter will obtain, although they cannot claim, possession of the whole, and the result will be a general indigestion, which nothing but a certain preparation of Tartar can remove: half a pound of the foul mixture would place our lives in imminent peril. Another uncomfortable effect of the ceremony is that in this case, as on all occasions where an Oriental sends you a present, a return is expected, and the amount of the return is supposed exactly to show at what rate you value yourself. We must give vails to all the fellows, otherwise we shall be called "fly-suckers," *i. e.*, skin-flints—a reputation which you, in your own country, and in these days, seem rather to court than to avoid, Mr. Bull; but what the East is not yet sufficiently enlightened to appreciate. We must also send a "token" to the noble giver of the sweetmeats; if we withhold it, he will not be too shamefaced to apply for it in person. I remarked that, during the visit, he repeatedly admired your ring, a bloodstone, with the family crest, a lion rampant, upon it. Send it to him, with an epigrammatic compliment, which I will impromptu for you, and you will earn, as the natives say, a "great name."

* * * *

"Well, Hari Chand, how progresses the Ameer?"

"The Ameer? Your exalted intelligence will understand most prosperously, only he has robbed his Ryot of all their camels, and now he is quarrelling with the neighbouring Jagirdars (country gentlemen), in order to get theirs to cheat the Company with; he has depopulated the land of small birds to feed his twenty hawks; he has been to Hyderabad and has returned stark-staring mad, swearing that he drank two sahibs under the table, and made love to every madam* in the place (Hari Chand is determined to excite our *ghairat*, or jealousy on that point by perpetually hammering at it); he has married another wife, although people say he has five† already; the new one being a devil, fights with all the old ones, who try to poison her; and his eldest daughter, when on a visit to the capital, ran away with a mounted policeman. Wah! wah! Verily, it is a noble family, as the poet said of the people of Cabul—

> "'A most distinguished race are they,
> The men can't say 'yes,' the women can't say 'no."'‡

"And Kakoo Mall?"

"Oh, Kakoo Mall! He is making a fortune by

* European ladies in general.

† Four wives are allowed by law and religion, but if a man marries half-a-dozen or so, it is considered a peccadillo, not a felony.

‡ Which by-the-by is borrowed from the Arab saying concerning the city of Wasit.

sedulously practising all kinds of iniquities. Praised be Allah! what a scoundrel he is! It would take hours to sketch out his villainies even for the exalted intelligence of your honours to comprehend them. But one of these days Kakoo must and will come to a bad end, a very bad end, which may be a warning to mankind."

This prediction, Mr. Bull, is simply the result of envy on the part of Hari Chand, who would give one of his eyes for the unlimited powers of doing evil, that good (to himself) might come of it, which he represents Kakoo Mall to enjoy. Of course he alludes piously to the vengeance of the gods; but the reference is an habitual one; the heart knows nothing about what the tongue speaks.

Ut sit magna, tamen certe lenta ira deorum est,

is a sentiment which misleads the Eastern as well as the Western would-be criminal. These people theoretically own the idea of retribution in this certain life; practically, they act as if sure to evade it. An unseen, an uncertain punishment has so little effect when threatened from afar! Offended Heaven may so easily be propitiated by vain oblations, and equally vain repentance. And, after all, celestial vengeance so often comes too late—a man may enjoy himself so many years before the blow descends! So they never neglect to threaten one another with the *ira deorum*, and always sin in the teeth of it themselves.

* * * *

Here is the Sawari, the retinue. Meer Ibrahim Khan, all crimson and gold, alights from his steed, a handsome Beloch mare, whose bridle and head-gear are covered with grotesque silver ornaments, and stands a moment patting her, to show off her points and equipments. The saddle is richly mounted,—though far inferior to those used by some of the petty Indian princes, whose led horses are decked in harness plated with precious metals studded with diamonds,—and there is no deficiency, at the same time no particular attraction, in the abundance of girth, housing, martingale and crupper, with which a gentleman's animal in this part of the world must be lumbered.

Ibrahim Khan prepares for dinner by dismissing all his attendants but one, Kakoo Mall, who remains to "toady" his highness, to swear the truth of every falsehood the great man tells, to supply him with an idea or a word whenever conversation does not flow glibly, and to be insulted, "chaffed" and derided, *tour à tour*, as the ill-humour or joviality of his chief prevail. The Ameer's quick glance has detected that we have nought but ale and cognac to offer him; that point settled, he assures his mind by feeling the smooth insides of our wine-glasses, by taking up the spoons, avoiding their handles, by producing brown facsimiles of his thumbs upon the white surface of the salt, by converting the mustard-pot into a scent-bottle, and by correcting any little irritation of the epidermis with our only corkscrew.

"Will you take a glass of the water of life, Meer Sahib?"

Perhaps, Mr. Bull, you expect our visitor to drink a few drops of brandy, as the French take *un petit verre d'absinthe pour ouvrir l'appetit.* If so, a quarter of an hour will convince you of your mistake.

Ibrahim Khan hands his gold-hilted sabre to the Affghan servant—who receives it at a distance, as if it bit, with a sneering smile for which he shall presently receive well-merited correction—sees it deposited in the corner of the tent, and then seating himself heavily upon the edge of the cot of honour opposite the dinner-table, he clutches a tumbler, blows warmly into it, polishes the damped interior with his pocket-handkerchief, and prepares to attack the liquid part of his meal.

We must join him if you please. In Scinde men drink before, in England after, dinner. At home, the object, we say, is to pass time pleasantly over a glass of wine: here, they honestly avow they drink to get drunk, and wonder what makes you do the same, disclaiming all intention of doing it. The Eastern practice is admirable for securing the object proposed to itself; every one knows that half-a-bottle upon an empty stomach does the duty of two emptied under converse circumstances. Moreover, the Scindians declare, that alcohol before meals whets the appetite, enlivens the spirits, and facilitates digestion. Habit is everything. I should advise you, Mr. John Bull, to follow the Meer's example at humble distance; otherwise a portly old gentleman in a state of roaring intoxication, singing and speechifying, excited combativeness and general benevolence, may be the concluding scene of this feast of unreason.

The dinner passes off rapidly. Ibrahim Khan eats quite as much as he drinks. Not contented with scooping up masses of boiled rice, hard eggs, and unctuous stews, in his palm, now and then stripping a kabab-stick* with his fingers, and holding up a large bone to his mouth with both hands, he proposes after our example to practise the knife and fork. With these articles, the former in the left, the latter in the right fist, he attempts to dissect a roast fowl, which dances away from him, as if it had vitality, over the damask, to the tune of loud hor! hors! Again he tries—again he fails, although he prefaced the second attempt by a Bismillah: "Heathen dog (to Kakoo Mall), is the soul of thy father in this bit of carrion?" for which gross insult † the Hindoo mentally fines his lord a thousand rupees, to be cheated the first opportunity. At last, desperate by the failure of many efforts, he throws away the fork, transfers the knife to his right hand, and grasping with his left the animal's limbs, he tears it piecemeal with a facility which calls for a loud explosion of mirth.

I never yet saw an Oriental laugh at himself so readily. Generally speaking, child-like, they are nervously and uncomfortably sensitive to ridicule of all kinds. Nothing offends them more lastingly than

* Bits of roast meat with onion between, fastened together with a skewer.

† Fowls are considered impure in the extreme, by high-caste Hindoos.

a caricature, be it the most good-natured. A writer of satire in Persia rarely dies an easy death; and the present race must be numbered amongst things that were, before a man could edit, at Teheran, a number of "Punch," and live through the day.

Scindian cookery is, like the country and its natives, a link between the Iranian and the Indian systems. Central Asia is pre-eminently the land of good living, and of masterly *artistes*, men as truly great in their exquisite art, as Paris or Naples ever produced: it teems with enjoyment to the philosophic *bon vivant*, who will apply his mind to naturalising his palate. Amongst the Hindoos, the *matériel* of the *cuisine* is too limited, consequently there is a monotony in the succession of rice dishes and vegetables: moreover, the bilious ghee enters into almost every preparation, the sweets are cloying, and the profuse spices annoying to the tasteful palate. In Scinde there are dawnings of culinary light, which would in a happier moral clime usher in a brilliant day. You have seldom eaten anything better—I will answer for the fact, Mr. Bull—than a *salmi* of black partridge, with a garnishing of stewed *bengans* or egg-plants.

The repast ends more abruptly than it began. The Scindian, as the boa constrictor, is always torpid after his ample meal, and he holds to the apothegm of the Salernitan school—

Post prandium est dormiendum.

You may observe our guest's fat heavy eyelids winking and drooping with progressive somnolency as the time for his *siesta* draws nigh. He calls for a cup of lukewarm milk,—the invariable and offensive conclusion to dinner here—apologises for leaving us, he must go to his prayers and attend to his guest-house,* promises a return to tea in the evening, calls for his horse, mounts it and retires.

Now that he is gone, perhaps you also, sir, may have "letters to write."

* * * *

"Ibrahimoo was so full of wine," remarks Hari Chand, "with these eyes I saw him almost tumble over his animal. He go to pray! he went to prepare for the evening's work. As for his guest-house, it is called by all the poor around, 'House of Hunger.'

* The wealthy nobles in Scinde generally support an establishment called Mehman-Khana, (guest-houses) in which they receive and entertain poor travellers and strangers.

Your honours, I hear, gave him only beer and brandy. You will see him presently return with a donkey's load of bottles. And I am told that he is going to bring his eldest boy; ah, your honours must button up your pouches now!"

* * * *

Here comes the Ameer with some additions to his former escort, Kakoo Mall; a little brown boy five or six years old, a minstrel, and a servant carrying many "grey beards."

In few parts of the world do you see prettier children than those of the higher class in Scinde. Their features are delicate and harmonious, the forehead is beautifully *bombé*, the full rounded cheek shows almost olive-coloured by the side of the silky black curls, and there is an intelligence and a vivacity which you scarcely expect to see in their large, long, lustrous black eyes. Their forms are equal to their faces: for symmetry and finish they might serve as models to the well-provided Murillo or Correggio. And the simplicity of their dress, a skull cap, a little silk frock like a nightgown, confined with a waist shawl in which sticks the tiniest of daggers, and a pair of loose slippers, contrasts most advantageously with the dancing-dog costumes with which your good lady, Mr. Bull, invests her younger offspring, or the unsightly jackets and waistcoats conferred upon Billy when breeched. If you like their dress you will also admire their behaviour: the constant habit of society makes them companionable at an age when your progeny is fit for nothing but confinement in a loose box, called a nursery. The boy here stands before his father, or sits with him when ordered, more staidly than one of your adults would do: he listens with uncommon gravity to the conversation of his seniors, answers pithily and respectfully when addressed, and never requires to be lectured upon the text, "Little children are made to be seen and not heard." At eight years of age he is master of the *usages*, he will receive you at the door in the absence of his progenitor, hand you to your proper seat in the room, converse with you, compliment you, call for pipes, offer you sweetmeats, invite you to dinner, and dismiss you without failing in a single point. As a boy he is a little man, and his sister in the harem is a little woman. This you may object to on the score of taste; say that it robs childhood of its chief charm, the natural, the innocent, and all that kind of thing. At any rate, you must own that it also preserves us from the very troublesome displays of the said charm in the form of pertness, selfishness, turbulence, and all the unlovely details comprehended in your "naughtiness"—the Irish "boldness."

Our admiration of their children is reciprocated by the Orientals. I have heard of a chief travelling many miles to see the fair face and flaxen hair of a "European baby;" and "beautiful as a white child" is almost a proverb amongst the dark-skinned Maharattas.

We must treat Master Ibrahim—I beg his pardon, Meer Jan Mohammed Khan Talpur, as he sententiously names himself—with especial attention as a mark of politeness to his father; we insist upon his sitting down, upon the highest seat too, inquire with interest after his horse and his hawk, look at his dagger, and slip in a hope that he may be as brave a soldier as his father. But we must not tell him that he is a pretty boy, or ask him his age, or say anything about his brothers and sisters, otherwise we offend against the *convenances*. And when we wish him to be sent home,—that venerable maxim,

> Maxima debetur puero reverentia,

is still venerated in the East—we give him a trifling tohfeh (present), a pocket pistol, or a coloured print, and then he will feel that the object of his mission has been fulfilled. In Central Asia, a child's visit is a mere present-trap.

You admire the row of bottles displayed upon the table, a dozen at least of champagne and sherry, curaçoa and noyau, brandy and gin, soda-water and pale ale. You will wonder still more when you see Ibrahim Khan disposing of their contents recklessly, mixing them (after consumption) by tumblers full, intoxicating himself each draught, and in each twenty minutes' interval, becoming, by dint of pushing his cap off his brow, scratching his head, abusing his moonshee, and concentrating all the energies of mind and body upon his pipe, sober as judges are said to be.

A faint "twang-twang," draws your attention to the corner of the tent. As in the ages preceding Darius, so since his time the *soirée* of oriental Cæsar or chief, never ended without sweet music.

Remark the appearance of the performer. He is a dark chocolate-coloured man with a ragged beard, an opium look, sharp, thin features, and a skin that appears never to have known ablution. A dirty torn cloth wrapped round his temples acts as turban: the rest of the attire, a long shirt of green cotton, and blue drawers, is in a state which may be designated "disgusting." In his hand is his *surando*, the instrument of his craft, a rude form of the violin, with four or five sheep-gut strings, which are made to discourse eloquent music by a short crooked bow that contains half the tail of a horse. He is preparing to perform, not in the attitude of a Paganini, but as we see in old Raphaels, and occasionally in the byways of Italy; the instrument resting upon his lap instead of his collar bone. Before the preliminary scraping ends, whilst the Meer is reviling Kakoo Mall *sotto voce*, a word or two about the fellow and his race.

The Langho, or as he is politely and accurately termed, the *Manganhar*, or "asker;"*—they are the most peremptory and persevering of beggars—is a particular caste in Scinde. Anciently, all the great clans had their own minstrels, whose duty it was to preserve their traditions for recital on festive occasions, and to attend the chief in battle, where they

* To call a man "beggar," does not sound polite in English, but it does in Scinde ears. An Oriental would generally prefer being under any kind of obligation to his superiors, than lack connection with them.

noted everything with an eagle's eye, praising those that fought, and raining showers of curses, taunts, and invectives upon those that fled. This part of their occupation is now gone. In the present day, they subsist principally by the charity of the people, and by attending at the houses in which their professional services at marriages and other ceremonies are required. They are idle as well as fond of pleasure, dirty, immoral, and notoriously dishonest. Largesse to a minstrel being a gentlemanly way of wasting one's substance in Scinde, those that employ the "asker," are provoked to liberality till either the will or the way fail. In the mean time, he spends every pice with all the recklessness of a western *artiste*, in drinking, gambling, and the silliest ostentation. He is not expected to live long, and none knows what becomes of him in his old age.

Our friend the Meer, has, I am told by Hari Chand, suffered so much from these men's sneering encomiums upon his valour and conduct in the late war, that he once tried the experiment of paying them liberally to avoid his palace. Finding that the revenues of Persia would be inadequate to carry out the scheme, he has altered his tactics, and now supports half a dozen of these, on the express condition that they never allude to the battles of Meeanee or Dubbah in his presence.

And now, as Ibrahim Khan looks tired of attempting to converse with our surly Affghans, and of outraging the feelings of his moonshee, we will lend an ear to music—heavenly maid, as she springs upon us in grimly guise from the head of Aludo, the minstrel.

The singing will commence with a favourite rhapsod theme—the murder of the great Lord Bahram, the ancestor of the Talpur Princes—by order of Sarfaraz, the Kalhora; and with the deadliest accuracy will it detail how an individual of lowly birth but brave, Shah Baharo, a Scindian, when ordered by the despot to do the deed, refused, saying, "I will fight the Beloch like a man." How Sarfaraz made light of Shah Baharo's chivalry and honour, asking "Where is Mohammed the Prophet of Allah, and where is Musaylimah the liar?"* How Shah Baraho responded with great temper and a prodigious quantity of good advice, the major part of which was *à propos* of everything; how Sarfaraz

* A false prophet, *i.e.* an unsuccessful one, contemporary with Mohammed. The phrase is a classical one amongst the Moslems; it is much used when drawing odious comparisons between man and man.

cozened and flattered till he found a willing bravo in Ismail Mombiyani the Scindian: how the said Ismail, being a one-handed man, cut down the valiant Bahram from behind with a sword which he held in his left hand raised a little higher than usual, and drew down the murdered chief's shoulder; how Ismail, after the assassination, cut off Bahram's head; and, finally, how Sarfaraz looked at it, and gave utterance to unchristian-like sentiments.

All the terrible minuteness of a French novel of the day or an Italian historical romance!

The sounds that accompany are more remarkable than the words of the song. Each fresh verse is ushered in by a loud howl so strikingly discordant that your every nerve starts at it, and so prolonged that anticipation wearies of looking forward to its close. To which follows the *Aria*, a collection of sharp chatterings, in a key strained at least two notes above the *voce di petto*, which, nevertheless, must be forced up to the mark, *falsetto* being unknown here: and, lastly, the conclusion of the phrase—a descent into the regions of the *basso* till the voice dies away, vaguely growling—lost, as it were, and unable to emerge from the depths into which it strayed. Then the howl, the chatterings, the soprano scream, and the growl over again. Half an hour of this work goes to the formation of a Scindian melody.

Melody!

Well, yes, melody! You see, sir, all around you are ecstatised, consequently there must be something to attract admiration in the performance. Of all the arts music is the most conventional. What do you think Orpheus would have thought of Thalberg —Thalberg of Orpheus? The traditions of all ancient people, Hindoos, Persians, Greeks, Romans, and others, tell of minstrels who worked miracles by the voice, the guitar, the lute, and the lyre. The music of the Greeks and Romans is beyond our reach; that of the Hindoo and the Persian is still in its old age, much the same, I should suppose, as it was when it began to exist. Accustomed to his own system, the Indian cannot derive the least pleasure from ours: the noisiness confuses him, his ear cannot detect a phrase, and he is ignorant of its harmony as he would be insensible to discord: he wonders greatly how it is that the European, so superior to him in arms and arts, can be so far behind in this one science, and he turns with eagerness to the strain familiar to his ear; not to the "Hindostanee melodies," which are occasionally composed in London, but to an honest, downright bit of barbarism, such as we have just now heard.

After my description, you will be astonished to hear that I could ever do anything but suffer during the endurance of the minstrel's song. At first all was pure torture. Presently, the ear in its despair began to make friends with the least harsh sounds, as prisoners do with spiders or jailers. Then, as a note or two became familiar, the utter strangeness wore off, and a sensation of grotesque enjoyment, novel and unexplainable, struggled into existence. At last, when a few years had thoroughly broken my taste to bear what you have just heard, I could listen to it not only without the horror you experience, but also with something more like gratification than composure. Possibly I like it better for the disgust it provoked at first. So the Highlander learns to love his screaming, wheezing, bagpipe; the German his putrescent *Sauerkraut*, the Frenchman *haut-goût* in game, the Italian his rancid olives, and all the world their snuff and cigars—

things which, at first they must, as they were human, have hated.

The songs generally sung by these Eastern jongleurs are legends, ballads, certain erotic verses which are very much admired by every class, and mystical effusions which the learned enjoy, and which the unlearned, being utterly unable to comprehend them, listen to with the acutest sensations of pleasure. The Homer of Scinde is one Sayyid Abdel Latif, a saintly bard, whose Risalo or collection of distichs upon traditionary themes of the two passions — love and war — has been set to different musical modes, and is, by the consenting voice of society, admitted to be a perfect *chef d'œuvre*, a bit of heaven on earth.

I will translate one of the songs which Aludo sings —a short satirical effusion, directed against the descendants of that celebrated man, by some Scindian poet, who appears fond of using the figure irony:

AN ODE TO THE HOLY MEN OF BHIT.*

I.

Ye monks of Bhit, whose holy care
Is fast and penance, wake and prayer!

* Bhit, is a small town lying to the eastward of Hyderabad. The word in Scindee literally means a "heap," and is applied to the place

Your lips and eyes bespeak a love
From low earth weaned to Heaven above!
Your hearts have rent all carnal ties,
Abjured all pomps and vanities!—
Not mean will be your meed I ken
In Heaven's bright realms, ye rev'rend men!

II.

And yet, they say, those tuneful throats,
With prayers' stern chaunt, mix softer notes;
Those mouths will sometimes deign to sip
The honey dew from maiden's lip;
And other juice than salt tear dyes
With purpling hues those heavy eyes,—
Ah! ah! twice blest your lot, I ken,—
Here, and hereafter—rev'rend men!

* * * *

You have a small musical snuff-box with you, Mr. John Bull, wind it up, put it in your pocket, and try the effects of a polka or a waltz.

All are silent in a moment. They start, stare, peer about the room, and look very much scared by the strange sounds. In another minute they will run away from us adepts in the black art. You see how many miracles could be got out of a few such simple

because the holy Abdel Latif ordered his followers to throw up a mound of earth there as a foundation for the habitations of men. The holy subjects of the Ode, although his descendants, have quite lost reputation amongst the Bards, because they ungenerously appropriated the hoards entrusted to their charge by the wife of the dethroned Kalhora prince. Perhaps being very wealthy, they are become as might be expected, very niggardly, and that is another cause of offence.

contrivances as a grind organ, an electrical machine, or a magic lantern. Now produce the cause of astonishment whilst I attempt to explain the mechanism of the invention. The sight of something soothes them; their minds become comparatively speaking quiet: still they handle the box with constraint, as if it had the power of stinging as well as singing. All are vociferous in praise of the music, probably on account of the curiosity of the thing, as a civilised audience applauds a sonata upon one string, at which it would yawn if performed upon four. Even the minstrel declares with humble looks that the charm has fled his *Surando*—that his voice is become like to the crows. This, however, is his politeness, not his belief. In what part of the world, or at what epoch of the creation, did a painter, a musician, or a poet, ever own to himself that he is a dauber, a mar-music, or a poetaster?

Ibrahim Khan will by no means refuse a "dish a tea," especially when offered to him during a short account of the Chinese Empire; the beardless state of the Celestials and the porcelain tower being topics which will at once rivet his attention. Orientals in their cups love to become inquisitive, scientific, theological and metaphysical. But he qualifies the thin potation with quite an equal quantity of brandy, as in his heart of hearts he has compared the first sip to an infusion of senna disguised by sugar and milk. The Belochies, unlike their neighbours the Persians and Affghans, are not accustomed to the use of *Chahi*.*

* * * *

"Meer Ibrahim Khan Talpur, listen! The meetings of this world are in the street of separation. And truly said the poet that the sweet draught of friendly union is ever followed by the bitter waters of parting. To-morrow we wander forth from these pleasant abodes, to return to Hyderabad. My friend Jan Bool Sahib is determined to feast his eyes upon the Adens of Larkhana and to dare the Jehannums of Shikarpur."—

The chief rises steadily though intoxicated.

"You are the kings of the Franks: you are the best of the Nazarenes, and, by the blessed Prophet, you almost deserve to be Moslems! Swear to me that you will presently return and gladden the glance of amity. What is life without the faces of those we love!

* Tea.

Wah! Wah! I have received you badly. There are no dancing-women in my villages: I would have seized a dozen of the Ryots' wives, but Kakoo Mall said—didn't you, you scoundrel?"

"Certainly, great chief!"

"How can the haiwans,* the Scindees, venture to show their blackened† faces in the presence of those exalted lords? If I have failed in anything, pardon me."

The tears stand in Ibrahim's eyes. No wonder. He has nearly finished six bottles. He grasps our hands at every comma, at every full stop vigorously embraces us. Yet he is not wholly maudlin. To water the tree of friendship as he phrases it, he stuffs my cheroot case into one pocket, and a wine glass into the other. I must give him your musical box, Mr. Bull, and as an equivalent—I don't wish him to go home and laugh at our beards—I gently extract his best hunting-knife from his waistband and transfer it to my own, declaring that with that identical weapon will I cut the throat of a poetic image called Firak or Separation.

* In Arabic, "anything that hath life"—popularly used to signify a beast as opposed to a human being, or a human being that resembles a beast.

† Blackened, *bien entendu*, by certain unquenchable flames.

Now the adieus become general. The minstrel raises his voice in fervent prayer—he has received five rupees and a bottle of bad gin. All the followers put their heads into the tent to bless us, and to see if we have anything to give them. The Ameer convinced that there are no more presents to be distributed, prepares to depart accompanied by his secretary, when Hari Chand determined upon a final scene, raises the tent-fly and precipitates himself into Kakoo Mall's arms.

* * * *

There is nothing in the south-east of Hyderabad which you have not seen before; a silt flat, sometimes sand, overgrown with desert shrubs, and here and there cultivated, huge heaps of ruins, long lines of water-courses, and channels, which become rivers during the inundation and widen into estuaries as they approach the ocean.

CHAPTER XXII.

THE MIMOSA BANK; ITS GIANT FACE.—SCINDIA. PETRÆA.—THE BELOCH MUSE.

Another month has passed away in grateful ease—doing nothing.

I would willingly lead you off Mr. Bull to the quondam University of Matara, and there lecture you on the present state of science and education in the Moslem world generally, and the Scindian in particular. I should like to accompany you to Nussarpoor and point out why some believe it to be the Mansureh of the Arabs, and why some believe as blindly that it is not Mansureh. I might even—had I my own way—start off with you to the eastern desert and amidst the mud walls of Omerkot expatiate upon the romantic events—such as the birth of Akhbar, its celebrity as a treasury, and its surrender without a shot to the British army,—which have, or ought to have, given it a name in universal history. Only I fear the habits of gaping, of setting down your neighbour a monomaniac, and of complaining that your expectations have been unwarrantably raised to be dropped—all which, dear sir, allow me to say, are now become highly natural to you. I must, however, as your guide, insist upon your accompanying me across the river westward to a certain spot called the Babbur Band or Mimosa Bank, in order to show you the prospect of the baldest desolation which our Unhappy Valley affords.

* * * *

We have been ferried over the Indus, and are travelling by easy marches northward, along the right bank of the great stream. Our two stages are, 1. Badha, nine miles from Kotree. 2. Onurpoor, twelve miles from Badha—Scindian villages and "that 's all."

We now strike off nearly due west, through a wild country, into one of the rugged little ranges of hills that extend like spider's legs from the main body of Alp, the Halah or Beloch mountains. Our two halting places are:—1. Lakra, twelve miles from Onurpoor. 2. Sibt, eight miles from Lakra—wells in the desert.

The rough and precipitous path zigzags most unartfully up, over and down the nakedest of stony ridges. The rocky face of the country suggests the idea that it is suffering under a complex attack of incurable cutaneous diseases. Here is a gigantic blotch—black leprosy—stretching many square miles without a shrub, much less a tree, for the stray bird of the wild to perch upon. There, after a long canter, we come upon a port-wine mark, a bit of ferruginous plain, most unlovely in its rustiness to all but the mineralogist's eye. Then again signs of white leprosy appear in flakes of glittering gypsum, washed down by the torrents from the declivities of the hills. The gangrenous hue of copper then attracts your eye. And lastly, though anxious to avoid any more of these unpleasant comparisons, you cannot but see an eternal jaundice in the rood after rood, scattered over with ton after ton of dirty yellow sulphur.

Apropos of this sulphur. Some years ago an enthusiastic seeker of mineral and other wealth, who penetrated into those hills, gathered promising looking specimens of it, and forwarded them to the officer commanding at Kurrachee, as a hint that the mines might be worked to advantage. But unfortunately the high authority was a Scotchman, and the colonel of a Highland Regiment: he resented the offer with a viciousness which strangled the project at its birth. Alas, Mr. Bull, how many schemes for benefitting mankind have been rendered abortive by a similar little accident of unskilfulness on the part of the operator!

As we advance we enter a long, wide, winding valley, bounded by a sandstone wall, whose crest time has cut into peaks and clefts of singular irregularity. The gently sloping sole and the general appearance of the ravine suggest an opinion that the waters of some deluge must have forced a passage through this pass from the plateau above, to the plains lying below the hills. A *fiumara* threads with frequent bends the deepest part of the declivity. You can see its character in its aspect. A few wild plants of the liveliest green spring from the margin of the bed, the course is strewed with blocks and boulders, immoveable except by tremendous violence, and down its centre—there has been a shower amongst the mountains—already gushes an angry brawling stream. On both sides of the channel, where its waters extend not, the furious summer heats have gashed the ground with many a gaping earth-crack; and except a straggling line of stunted mimosas, rough and wild-looking as the land that bears them, there is nothing but the "shadow of the great rock" as the Hebrew beautifully has it, to protect the traveller's throbbing head from a sun which even at this season of the year glows like a globe of living fire.

You will not be astonished to hear that this is a haunted spot. The legends of the country inform us that it is tenanted by a Giant Face, the remains of some pagan magician whose head was spared whilst his form was consigned to the flames below. Its terrible eyes are, they say, ever fixed upon those of the wayfarer; they are eternally before him, whether he advance or retire, turn to the right or to the left, lie prostrate or lie prone; vainly he strives to escape them.

We unbelievers are not likely to see it; yet, uncouth as the fancy is, we own it—not in our comfortable well-lit studies, but when wending our way through the dim starlight of the scene—a strong superstition, not strange, but rather based upon a known foundation.

Did you ever, Mr. Bull, when abandoned by your

nurse to the horrors of a big black bedroom, see a grinning face advance towards you from the distant apex of the huge cone which lay before your closed eyes—advance gradually, but unavoidably, till, in spite of your struggles, its monstrous features were so close to yours, that you could feel them; then, almost suddenly, start back from you, flit away, diminish till nothing but the dark eyeballs remain in sight, and disappear presently to return with all its terrors? If you did, you may understand what I mean by calling this a strong superstition.

We will say nothing, if you please, about the Giant Face before our servants. It is sufficient to frighten the boldest Affghan half out of his wits.

* * * *

There *are* men and women, you would hardly believe it, on these stones. Those heaps of natural slabs, piled up against the hill-sides, are their graves. And although your unpractised eye cannot detect them, I can here and there catch sight of the tall limber spear of some herdsman sheltering himself under a ledge of rock or concealed behind a line of rising ground. The people are partly Scindian, partly Beloch: both are equally savage and ferocious.

We now travel, however, under the formidable escort of a name—the Devil's Brother, as H. E. the Governor is dutifully called by his subjects, being our protection. Ten years ago, we should have required twenty or thirty horsemen to force this pass, and then we should not have succeeded without a a little "sniping" at every spot favourable to the unpleasant sport. As it is, our men, most of them born plunderers, temporarily reclaimed, are talking about a fortalice of camels. This barbarous variety of field-works is formed by seating the animals in a circle, with their heads inside, their quarters placed to stop the balls, and their knees tied and tethered,—to obviate the danger of a breach being made in the curtain of the barbican, by part of it leaping frantically from the ground;—whilst the defenders are ensconced behind the inner round of loads and packsaddles which forms the ballium. Such precaution, however, thanks to our general, is quite unnecessary now.

Two miles beyond Sibt, is the Mimosa Bank, or rather the place where it used to be. It was a line of earth and stones thrown across the narrow neck of the valley, causing the rains and torrents to inundate the plateau instead of flowing down the *fiumara* directly to the Indus. The rent which last spring made in its side is nearly two hundred feet long: the foundation is so bad, and the power pressing upon the work is so great, that there is little chance of repairing it with permanent success. A glance at the plain beyond will convince you that water in these regions is all in all.

*   *   *   *

You see, Mr. Bull, a Beloch family of the noble house of Rind: quite a different people, as their looks tell, from the half-Scindian porpoises, like Ibrahim Khan, settled on and about the Indus. Their features, though comely in youth, are strongly marked and unpleasant in mature manhood and age; their figures are unexceptionable, straight, muscular, and symmetrical; as for their dress, it is a long wide robe of unbleached canvas, buttoned at the throat, the same as that worn amongst the wild Arabs before the days of Noah; they twist a fold of cotton round the temples to guard them from the sun, and to confine the long grisly bushes of black hair which cloak their shoulders with wild curls; undergarments they have none, and the only protection afforded to their feet against the flints of the hill and the thorns of the plain, are slippers made with the leaves of a dwarf palm. The men show little fear, the women less shame, in our presence; they have heard that we are not likely to steal their goats, asses, and pony, and they have nothing to lose besides these and themselves. Had they been Scindians, they would have fled from their own well in terror. But they are "sons of the Beloch," that is to say, of thieves and soldiers, as they will tell us: so, with a fellow-feeling which we cannot reject even though we object to it, they will sit with us under the thicket in the *fiumara* bed, admire us whilst we eat breakfast, tempt us to knock over a butcher-bird or two flying, consider us a low order of demi-god, and assist in pitching our tent with the honourable regard for the distinctions of "mine" and "thine," said to flourish amongst members of the old profession. A glass of gin will bribe them to return in the evening and help us to pass it by means of a *Saringi* and a song. Look at their homes—a clump of little low tents of sable felt upon a dwarf gallows of three poles. Travellers are wont to chronicle their lusting to see, and their heart-jumpings when first seeing, these "black tents." You remark that it is very like a gipsy's encampment, Mr. Bull! I feel almost inclined to leave you *planté*.

The Beloch, according to his own account, is an emigrant from Aleppo and the adjacent provinces. Asiatic ethnologists derive him from the Arabs of Hejaz; but his language is of the Indo-Persian, not the Semitic, family, and his appearance bears little resemblance to that of Ishmael's descendants. The eye is the full, black, expressive Persian,—not the small, restless, fiery Arab organ; the other features are peculiarly regular and Iranian; and the beard, unerring indicator of high physical development, is thick and flowing. The race occupies a large portion of the Halah mountains and the provinces, as Mekran, Kerman, Kohistan, Seistan, and others contiguous; it has spread far and wide over the different parts of Central Asia, even as far south as Muskat; and the reputation of being brave and faithful soldiers seldom leaves these Switzers of the East destitute of honourable employment.

As regards character, the hill Beloch has all the nomadic virtues of morality, hospitality, simplicity, strong affections, fidelity, stubborn courage, and a bigoted attachment to the faith of his forefathers. At the same time, he has in equal proportion all the nomadic vices—sanguinary ferocity, barbarous ignorance, the wildest passions, an insane spirit of revengefulness, and a love of plundering which knows no bounds. The blood feud was as actively at work in these mountains when we took them as in the wilds of Arabia: even Sir Charles Napier found difficulty in persuading a chief to forgive him an indefinite man owed by the head of a rival tribe. Such is their inborn love of robbery, that, in "the good old times," the wealthiest Sardar would sometimes take to the highway, disguised, merely for the sake of adventure. Their women are their facsimiles, only, as usual, a little more instinctive and a little less reasonable, more prone to excess and less capable of comprehending what "golden mean" signifies. The Beloch has learned better than to follow the traditionary precept of his prophet—

Shaviruhunna wa Khalifuhunna.*

He treats his wife in every way as his equal, and he readily owns that much more villainy can be per-

* "Take counsel of them, (feminines,) and then do exactly the contrary of what they advise you to do." Certainly that prophet had a habit of saying strange things.

petrated with, than without, the able assistance of a lady's wit. Whereas his brother on the plains, who has picked up a few sentiments from Hafiz and Sadi, in his unaffected contempt for, his perfect atheism in the "rights of woman" and the "purity of the sex," matches any Hindoo Pundit that ever sat down to overwhelm the daughters of Eve with the weight of defamation in Sanscrit verse and prose.

The Beloch emigrated to the low country about the middle of the last century, in consequence of an invitation from the Kalhora Prince of Scinde, who, like an old husband, chose the very intimate he should have avoided. He has had time to degenerate. To many of his old defects, ignorance, violence, and brutishness of manner, he has added new and worse ones. He has learned to lead a life of indolence, and to consider all the animals around him, wife and fellow creatures, created to serve him. He has lost the merriment and appreciation of a joke which his mountain kinsman possesses—none of his contempt for any art higher than the training of a horse, or the flying of a falcon. Stupid and apathetic to the last degree, he delights in intoxicating preparations, and wallows in the mire of debauchery, which accompanies the free use of stimulants in the East. As a soldier, he will boast invincibly, fight pretty well under the influence of opium, and run away as readily as do those whom shame and not "game" makes to fight. He is without skill in the use of arms: as a matchlockman inferior to the Affghan, as a swordsman to the Arab, as a spearman to the Hindoo, and of the Persian jereed he knows nothing. Yet it would be hard to find a match for the swaggering ferociousness of his gait, heightened and set off by the small armoury of weapons, sabre and dagger, matchlock and misericorde, pistol, spear, and shield, belt and ball pouch, powder flask and primer, with which Bobadil purposes, single handed, to do the work of a host.

* * * *

Here they come, ladies and gentlemen: the former bestriding lean ragged Yaboos,* the latter their favourite chargers. Mares are preferred to horses, on account of their superior endurance, their docility, and their not being in the habit of neighing. Formerly, when chupaos or raids into the low country formed the business of a highlander's life, the quality of silence was not less valued than that of tractability.

* Stout shaggy ponys for riding or carrying burdens.

It is a favourite Beloch proverb, that a robber with his saddle on a mare, has his saddle on a horse, whereas, that a robber with his saddle on a horse, has his saddle on his head.* The animals are lean and ill-favoured, especially when in training; but, in spite of their weedy looking limbs, the eye and the nostrils, the silky coat, and bunching muscles, show that good and pure blood flows in their veins. They are tame as dogs to their owners, and possess, to a considerable extent, the courage and presence of mind, if I may use the expression, which the Arab holds to be the true test of quadruped blood. In perseverance they are indomitable. Nothing can be more ragged or miserable than their equipments, a bridle of cord with a jagged bit of iron used for a snaffle, and a bare wooden saddle whose seat reminds you of an obsolete instrument of military punishment. Few Europeans would reach the end of a short stage, on a Beloch mare, without feeling the effects of it for a week ; the owner, however, will travel sixty, seventy, or eighty miles on her back, through a burning sun, without a halt or a drop of

* Meaning that he will probably have to carry the saddle home on his head. In order to plunder a village you must dismount, and nine or ten animals must be entrusted to a single pair of hands. If they are horses they are sure to fight, and to break away from the holder ; not so when mares.

water, and consider the feat a morning's ride. The pace preferred is the amble, occasionally varied by a long loose canter: the beasts are accustomed to keep it up over the most dangerous paths, and as for slopes and hills, they ascend and descend them more like goats than horses.

I cannot say that I admire the ladies' style of equitation in that somewhat too simple attire of theirs. At the same time, Mr. Bull, I must observe that, with all its faults, it is less unsightly—in my humble opinion—and certainly less dangerous than the habit of hanging suspended on a peg, half off the animal's side, with a train ready to catch everything that comes in its way. Now, however, your ladies have associated their peculiar seat, and their over-grown petticoats, with their "modesty," so that a word against them will be a personal reflection, to be met with counter-personalities. But, perhaps, your granddaughter, when she sees how truly becoming are a pair of large rich shalwars, or petticoat-trowsers, and she feels how safe the man's seat is, will

—"all for new-fangledness of gear,"

discard her ridiculous habit, and once more ride as nature intended her to do. Lady H. Stanhope tried the experiment with success. I was told by an eye-witness that nothing could be more correct than her appearance—astride. It is strange, when one reflects about it, that the European lady on horseback must preserve the only troublesome, unsightly, and dangerous part of her dress, when she exchanges her bonnet for a hat, wears a cravat, and buttons up her fair bust in what much resembles a shell jacket, still more the upper garment of a little foot-page or "buttons."

The ladies will retire to their romantic, uncomfortable abode, the black tents: they are not afraid of us, but "etiquette"—odious word!—forbids them to sit with the men in ours. Our only chance of amusement is from the bhat or bard—that individual with fierce features, and eyes rolling in a fine frenzy, produced, I fear, by sundry draughts of gin, with which our servants have been privately plying him. His instrument is a dried gourd, with a handle to form notes, and three strings of brass wire, which produce sounds that twang like the whizzing of an angry hornet's wings. Such is the ambur of the hills.

The language of these mountaineers is the

Belochki, either a barbarous corruption, or more probably an unpolished cognate dialect of that venerable and most beautiful tongue, the Persian. It is easily learned, as the vocabulary is meagre, being confined to the names of things; and the grammar is even less complicated than that of our own tongue. But it contains little or no literature; and the days are not come when "sharp young men" who aspire to become "politicals" turn their attention to it: so that with the exception of two or three enthusiastic linguists, we have heard it spoken and recited for the last ten years, without attempting to pick up a word of it. The effusions of our bard may not be uninteresting to you: only you will excuse my not attempting to fringe them with rhyme, or in any way to clothe them in a poetical dress, for the best of reasons—namely, that they are essentially prosaic.

The first specimen is of a devotional nature, a *véridique histoire*, usually impromptued *à loisir*, containing, as oriental poetry is so fond of doing, a moral or religious lesson, which at first sight appears no lesson at all. The apparent truism of the following is, that the Almighty is almighty: its inner sense I could explain in a Sermon by a Subaltern—if you would listen to it:—

THE TALE OF BARI AND ISA.

Give ear, O ye sons of the Beloch,
Whilst I recount to you a true tale!
As Isa, the prophet of the Lord,
Was travelling, fakir-like, over the earth,
Seeing its wonders and its wastes,
He came into a desert land
Where no river or kareez was—
No green fields, no waving crops.
Dreadful mountains rose on all four sides,
Round a plain of sand and flint,
On which stood a stump (of tree) one cubit high,
And propped against it sat Bari, the hermit,
Meditating with his shroud * over his head,
Upon the might of Rabb Taala.†
Isa considered him awhile,
Then, advancing, he touched his shoulder,
Saying, "Tell me truly, how dost thou live?
What eatest thou in this grainless place,
And what drinkest thou where no water is!"
Bari raised his head from his breast,
He was old and stone blind,
His knees were sore by continued kneeling,
And his bones through fasting pierced his skin:
Yet his heart was as the life of the seed
That dwells in a withered home.‡
He comprehended (the question) and thus replied,
Weeping and exclaiming, "Wa waila! §
"How can man doubt the Creator's might?

---

* A *momenti mori*, fashionable amongst Eastern devotees.

† The Creator.

‡ Meaning that his heart in his withered bosom was as the germ of life in the dry seed—a true Pythagorean oriental idea.

§ Wa Waila; "alas! and alas!" The exclamation, an Arabic one, is put into Bari's mouth on account of the sacredness of his character. Saints, prophets, and sages, are always made to speak as Semitically as possible.

Sit down by me for awhile,
I show thee the power of the Lord."
Then the stump shot up till it became
A noble towering tree ;
At morning prayers it began to grow,
And (presently) shadowed the ground beneath ;
At mid-day berries appeared upon it,
Hanging in festoons like the young brab's fruit.
In the afternoon they became brightly red,
As the date when it falls from the tree.
Before the sun set they were ripe :
From each bough the bunches hung
Cool as water in a cavern,
Sweet as the sugar * of paradise,
Fit for prophets and martyrs to eat.
Then said Bari, " Thou seest the Lord's might,
How He can feed His children in the waste !
Fruits grew upon the (withered) stump,
Waters flow from the rugged rock,
All things obey the Lord of all,
It is (only) man that doubts and disbelieves."
As it happened unto him,
So, by my head, may it happen to me.
Such is the tale of the Dervish,†
Gentles, my song is ended.

Nothing can better illustrate the intensity of

* In the days when sugar of any kind was a rarity, and consequently a delicacy, our English poets used the word with a certain appetite in their comparisons. Now the metaphor is apt to offend the sensitive ear long accustomed to associate the word with nursery discussions, or tiresome colonial grievances. But in the Persia, "Shakkar" (sugar) still holds its ground as a fit simile for things nice and dainty ; for instance, a "sugar-candy-chewing parrot" is a compliment which may be offered to the most fastidious dame in the land.

† The songs always conclude with some such formula as this.

clannish feeling amongst the mountaineers than the few following lines, which represent *the* Rind to be lord and master of all the other septs, who, moreover, are described to be so low and worthless, that the Rind's brother-in-law absolutely refused to take them as his bride's dowry. Were we philosophical (Scotch) Highlanders, Mr. Bull, some of these people's ideas would be highly interesting to us:

> The Kidds, the Gabols, the Gadhis, and the Pacholos,
> The Talpurs, and the lawless Murrees,*
> Were all *tout bonnement* † slaves to Chakar (*the* Rind).
> He gave them to his sister Banadi
> As her dowry, when she married Hadhiya;
> But the latter refused to take them,
> The slaves were so vile, &c., &c.

To conclude with a "tale of true love"—*à l'Irlandaise* so far that the hero carries off the heroine by main force, knocking, at the same time, every one he can on the head—*à la Beloch* in that, amidst all the transports of clasping to his bosom a charming bride, he by no means neglects to secure all the transportable goods and chattels—belonging to her paternal progenitor—upon which

* Names of Beloch clans.

† The Belochee, or rather Persian word, is "durust," which our language cannot render but by a periphrase.

he can lay his hands. By the effect which the song will produce upon the audience, you will decide that the bard has rightly chosen and skilfully handled his subject :

Endue my tongue, O Allah, with truth!
My love is a pigeon, a pea-hen in gait,
A mist-cloud in lightness, in form a Peri ;*
And her locks are like the tendrils of the creeping shrub.
Burned for her my heart with secret longing,
As the camel-colt, torn from his dam's side.
At length when the taste of life was bitter on my palate,
Came the old minstrel carrying his guitar ;
In his hand was a token from that lovely maid ;
Then my withered heart bloomed as the tree in spring,
And smiles of joy like the dawn lighted my brow.
"Come, come, my companions, ye lawless Beloch,
Whose fame for theft is great!
Bind on your high-priced swords!
Seize your pliant spears!
Loose your mares from their pickets and heel ropes,
Let them dance while you bind their head gear on,
And girth their saddles with the worked stirrup-irons!
Now ride we like ravening wolves
Towards the sheep-house, the low country!"
I mount my steed, whose ears are like reeds,
And push on bravely through the night,
Till, without halting, we arrive before dawn
At the flourishing Raj,† on the Pir-wah,

* This word is feminine in all the Indian dialects save one, the Multani, which admits a Perá, or male fairy.

† The generic name for a Scindian village in the wild parts of the country, situated we are told on one of the one hundred water-courses, bearing the name of Pir-wah—"Saint's-canal."

Where lives my fairest of maidens,
Amongst lovely dames in the reed huts.
I opened the curtains of her abode,
And crept in disguised in a beggar's blanket;
As the tree joys at the prospect of the blossom,
So expanded my heart with delight,
The torments of months left my heart.
Said my love, "How can I leave my mother,
For my father to heap curses upon her head?"
I wept raining showers of tears,
But her will was hard as the hills of the Beloch.
Then I seized her pliant form in my arms,
And with the end of my turban I stopped her mouth:
She struggled like the kid in the tiger's jaw,
But soon she rested her head on my shoulder.
Then came out the players of the sword-fight,
Gulzar, Sajalo, and Bahram the brave,*
With two hundred doughty warriors,
Spearsmen and bowmen, many a one.
We were sixty in all, thieves of renown,
Whose names were terrible in the low country.
Quickly we mounted and wheeled our steeds,
And shouted "Allah!" † and couched our spears,
And fell upon them smiting with our swords
The faces and jaws of the shielded foe,
Till many had fallen, and the rest fled
From the sight of our bay-coloured snorting mares.

* The names of the opposing Scindian warriors.

† The War-cry; these pious thieves never rob, save in the name of Allah. Moreover, they casuistically justify theft by making it a compulsory act of charity, demanding for instance your coat, and reproaching you with hard heart for seeing unmoved a fellow creature's semi-nudity. Observe that when fighting is on the tapis, the Bard forgets all about the lady, who poor thing has probably been thrown like a sack of corn across a yaboo, and driven off by some low fellow who cannot fight, to a temporary place of safety.

Then pushed we our beasts to speed,
And drove off all the camels and goats we could find.
That night the clouds refrained to rain,
The stars twinkled bright as maidens' eyes,
And the moon shone upon the stony path.
We came back unharmed to our resting place,
Where drums beat gladly to see us again.
We cast lots for the plunder with arrows and straws,
My bride was pleased with none but me,
She has forgotten her mother, her playmates, and her
    companions,
And walks with a dainty boy on her hip.
        Such is the tale of the bard,
Gentles! my song is finished.

We will hang a red cotton shawl round the bard's neck, in token of full approval, and dismiss our friends to their affectionate wives, children, and mares with a few presents of cheap finery. So shall the memory of our visit to these mountains endure for many a long year.

You need not hesitate to slumber in peace, Mr. Bull. The fellows have eaten our salt, and they are as true to that condiment as any Arab. Moreover, are we not, as I said before, under the vampire pinion of H. E., the Devil's Brother?

CHAPTER XXIII.

THE LUKKEE PASS, AND ITS EVIL SPIRIT.—SEHWAN, ITS BEGGARS AND ITS "ALEXANDER'S CAMP."

You may not be sorry to hear, Mr. Bull, that you have now seen the worst of our Unhappy Valley; all that remains is the grand, the pretty, and the picturesque—in fact Scindia Felix.

Four stages* from Onurpoor, along the right bank of the river—stages so utterly uninteresting that they hardly deserve a place in your diary—lead us to the little village of Lukkee, near the pass and the ridge of that name.

The hills appear to be almost within stone throw of our tent, but the clearness of the atmosphere takes from their distance: they are at least three miles off. The dead, yellow, alluvial flat—the creation of the

* Namely, Gopang thirteen miles; Manjdan fourteen; Sann twelve; and Amri twelve. These two are flourishing villages, especially the latter one; as materials for description they, and the districts adjacent to them, are abominations.

Indus—sweeping up to the eastern base, adds the majesty of height to their stature; they are scarcely twelve hundred feet above the level of the lowland—they seem to be three thousand. At a distance nothing can be more beautiful than the bluish-green tint—a mixture of air and Jawasi shrub*—which envelopes them: nothing grander than the forms of their fantastic peaks and pinnacles, the dark ravines streaking their huge flanks, their precipitous falls and their broad slopes, here shelving into the plain, there buttressing the mighty wall against the encroachments of the violent river. As we approach the foot, we remark a disposition of the strata, striking to the most ungeological eye. Huge layers of pebbles appear pitched upon their edges, and dovetailed into one another, sometimes in acute, sometimes in obtuse, angles, as if of yore a terrible convulsion of nature had heaved the original crust of earth high up in the air, and then breaking it into massy fragments, had left it exposed to view, the memento of her mighty sport.

We must visit the chief point of attraction in the Lukkee Hills, in spite of the trouble it will give us.

* The camel-thorn.

Our path leads towards a fissure visible from afar, a split in the heart of the mountain: the rocks on both sides raising their corresponding forms, at this distance, bleak and bare looking, against the unbroken hue of the firmament beyond. As we near the gloomy place, our admiration of its desolation increases. We dismount and toil slowly up, threading our way through blocks and boulders, which the action of the water has parted from their parent cliffs, and under impending masses, that frown as if the least pretext would make them fall and crush us. The dell narrows rapidly from two hundred to fifty feet, and the tall sides become perpendicular enough almost to exclude the soft light of the setting sun, whose last smile is reflected by the upper peaks with a lovely blush. Through the bottom of this black gash runs a hot and dingy rivulet, filling the air with closeness and fetid steam, as it swirls down its white chalky bed, coated over with sulphureous deposit. We approach its source, and the bubbling sound changes to a roar, heightened by the echoes that surround it, and the spray lights sensibly upon our toiling forms.

This, you may see by the many emblems of its

worship scattered about, is a place of Hindoo pilgrimage*—Dhara Tirtha, as they call it. The people have a goodly superstition connected with the scene. In the old time of Brahma's superiority it was a favourite spot for those acts of religious suicide, with which the Pagan ascetics loved to conclude the present form of existence. Whenever one of the order wished to ascertain from the Deity whether the time for his emancipation were come, he ascended to the source, and after ablution, prayer, and meditation, he prepared to pass the night upon that little platform of black rock. If terror deprived him of sleep, it was a sign from Heaven that the mortal coil was not to be shuffled off so suddenly; but if he slept composedly till morning dawned, that day was destined to witness his liberation from the world of matter, and the absorption of his soul into the Self-existent whence it was parted. One of the great trials of the devotee's faith was an apparition haunting the black cave, or rather hole, in the rock side opposite the platform. The ascetic, who, seduced by her beautiful form and harmonious accents, accepted her invitation to a *tête à tête*, was fated to

* The Moslems also consider it a holy spot.

die, like the lovers of preternatural ladies in general, painfully. But, on the other hand, when Fate willed mercy, an unseen arm of irresistible power arose to check him, as his body was toppling down headlong into the rocky bed of the sulphur stream.

Stop, Mr. Bull, I am thinking of Vaucluse—Nero's Baths—all manner of classicalities. And *entre nous,* old gentleman, I am rapidly growing poetical; so I should advise you, no amateur of such things, to leave me for a *petit quart d' heure* while the paroxysm expends itself:

* * * *

In awful majesty they stand,
Yon ancients of an early earth,
High towering o'er the lowly land
That in their memories had birth;
And spurning from their stony feet
The rebel tides, that rush to beat
And break where rock and water meet.
Hoar their heads and black their brows,
And scarred their ribbed sides, where ploughs
Old Age his own peculiar mark
Of uneffaceable decay;
And high and haughty, stern and stark—
As monarchs to whose mighty sway,
An hundred nations bow—stand they.

Within the deep dark cleft of rock dividing,
Two giants taller than their kin,

Whence the sharp edge of piercing torrent gliding,
Here flashes sudden on the sight, there hiding
'Mid stones all voice with crashing din,
Where earth-born shade with skylight blends,
A grot of grisly gloom impends
The source from which the wave descends.
Upon its horrid mouth, I ween,
The foot of man hath never been—
The foulest bird of prey would sink
To nestle on that noisome brink.
Now the warm cauldron's sulphury fumes upseething,
As sighs that Stygian pit exhales,
The cavern's pitchy entrance veils,
Then in the winds cold breath the vapours wreathing,
Dissolve—again the eye defines
The dripping portals' jagged lines.

A glorious vision from that cave,
Glittered before my gazing eye,
A seraph-face, like one that beams
Upon his sight, when blissful dreams
Round holy hermit's pillow fly
A form of light, as souls that cleave
The darksome dungeon of the grave,
When awful Judgment Hour is nigh.
And O, the voice! Can words express
The fullness of its loveliness,
Its rare and wondrous melody?
Ah, no—no mortal tongue may be
So powerful in poesy!
Might I but gaze upon that brow,
Might I but hear that witching strain,
The joys that all the Seven Climes * know,

* Moslems reckon seven climates on the earth; their "Haft-Iklim," therefore means this sublunary world. This is blending together two superstitious, but, *n' importe*.

The charms that all the Heavens show,
  Were mine—but mine in vain.

A moment pass'd the sound away,
Faded the vision from my sight,
And all was as it was before,
Vapour and gloom and deaf'ning roar.
Then arose that sound again—
Again appeared that form of light
Athwart the blue mist, purely white,
As from the main, at break of day,
Springs heavenwards the silv'ry spray.

She beckoneth to me,
And in that smile there is
Promise of love and bliss,
Enduring endlessly.

Whirled my brain, my heedless foot
  Already left the verge,
Where the water-spirit pours
  His bolts of feathery surge.
Where iron rocks—around—beneath,
Stand quick to do the work of death :
When suddenly an icy arm
  Against my falling bosom pressed ;
Its mighty touch dissolved the charm,
  As suns disperse the mists that rest
  On heathery mountains' dewy crest.
I heard the angry waters rave,
I saw the horrors of the grave.
    That yawned to gulf its prey,
And started back in such dismay,
As wretch that, waked from midnight sleep,
Descries through shadows, glooming deep,
The ghost of murdered victim glide,
In gory robes, his couch beside.

I looked towards the darksome cave,
No more the vision glittered there,
No music charmed the echoing air,—
That strain so sweet! That face so fair!—
And but for one shrilly shriek
Of fiendish rage that smote mine ear,
And but for one horrent thrill,
That seemed with ice my veins to fill,
I well had deem'd 'twas Fancy's freak,
That scene, whose vivid features lie
On memory's page typed durably.

*   *   *   *

It's all over, Mr. Bull.

Our morning's ride from Lukkee to Sehwan is about thirteen miles. The first third of the way lies across a plain, whose dimensions narrow rapidly as we advance. Then commences a straight defile of some length, with the crumbling precipitous bank of the rapid river on one side, on the other a perpendicular rock abruptly rising seven or eight hundred feet above our heads. A few years ago when Lord Keane's force marched up by this way, here was a long flat of alluvial formation covered with old and stately trees: now the river is almost ready to undermine the rocky wall which opposes it. In some places the defile is so narrow that our camels marching in Indian file look dangerously situated. Reaching the tip of this tongue of land, the road strikes abruptly leftwards, winding through a steep and rugged cleft in the last spur of the Lukkee mountains. Unless we wish to break our horses' knees, we had better dismount and lead them. There is also a view to look at, and you may be curious to see the miseries which our unhappy beasts of burden endure when compelled to place the soft cushions of their feet upon the rolling stones of the ascent.

Standing close to the police station,—which, with due allowance made for latitude and longitude, reminds me of many a little guard-house in that barbarous region the Apennines—we command a prospect of the plain below. The serpentine form of the Indus lying shrunken in its sandy bed, and unruffled by the least breath of wind, here glows crimson with the light of the rising sun, there screened from the horizontal rays flows like a line of quicksilver, pale as the face of the morning sky. Near, the lively green of the young tamarisks which overgrow the plain, breaks through the veil of thin vapour floating over the dewy earth: in the distance, lies a mass of bold hill, azure and gold above, darkly purple below, where it unites with the level ground.

Comical enough is the demeanour of those sagacious beasts, our camels. They measure the steep and scan the road with a mingled expression of curiosity and apprehension. The foremost halts, roars, curls his ugly little tail, and wheels round so abruptly as almost to ease himself of his burden: the rest of the line is thrown into confusion; box grating loudly against box, and bag violently flattened by bag. Ensues the usual scene. Nose-strings are spitefully clutched and jerked, quarters are unmercifully poked and belaboured, and a hundred curses are chattered in half the time it would take you to produce a dozen. And, as usual, the human brute wins the day. The unruly Ships of the Desert conquered and dejected with a *s'il faut il faut* expression on every feature come slowly clambering, slipping, and tottering up the path, roaring pitiably at the hard necessity, and chewing the cud between whiles, like hungry old ladies dining in a state of grievous affliction.

And now, after descending, we pass over a hillocky, sandy, rocky plain, about three miles in length, descry a mass of houses clustered at the base of a huge flat-topped mound, and in course of time find ourselves sitting in expectation of our tents, under the hospitable jujube trees of a Sehwan garden.

Sehwan, or as the place is more grandiloquently called, Sewistan, is, we must own, a city of some antiquity, disposed as our minds are by the exaggerations of the archæologists to deny everything deniable. It is mentioned by the native annalists as one of the six forts which the Hindoo rulers of Scinde were careful to garrison and repair. After the thirteenth century of our era it rose to distinction by the favour of a certain saint, to whose tomb we shall presently perform the traveller's pilgrimage. Of late years the place has declined in the scale of prosperity. At present nothing can be more miserable and dilapidated than the appearance of the town. Its streets are filthy amongst the filthy, and not even Coleridge himself could define and generalise the genera and species of its nauseous odours. And Sehwan the luckless, is likely to fall still lower. Formerly it was a place of some military as well as religious importance, commanding the passage of the Indus: now the river, its second great stand-by, is gradually deserting it. The climate is celebrated as the most deleterious and deadly of this miasmatic land: one glance at the hapless population is proof palpable of its effects upon the body and mind of man. And, as is the case, I believe, in all sacred places and holy cities, from Rome to Mecca, the inhabitants are a very disreputable race.

* * * *

On our way to the tomb you will easily remark on the principal peculiarities of the town.

We are surrounded as soon as sighted by a host of pauper cripples, the young and old of both sexes: at every turn a knot of beggars, obstructing our way, adds a few units to the throng; every one is a mendicant it would appear; the very babies look impatient to begin begging. This gentleman deserves your special notice. He is a Kalandar*—a Calendar, as those dear old Frenchified Arabian Nights do so delightfully confuse the word—and an excellent specimen of his class is he. His long matted filthy locks are crumpled up under a greasy felt thing, formed like a western fool's cap, his neck, arms, and legs, are bare, and a woollen cloth, pepper and salt,

* This Arabic word is properly applied only to a Sufi, or Mystic, who works out his own salvation without the guidance of a spiritual master. The effect of which independence of spirit is generally to produce a reprobate of distinction.

purposely fashioned like a shroud to show how dead the scoundrel is to the pomps, vanities, *et cetera*, covers his gaunt angular carcase. In one hand he carries a rosary whose every bead is the size of a boy's "taw;" in the other the cup of dried gourd, from which he pours forth libations to Bacchus, and in which he receives the alms of the charitable: under his arm is a huge black wood bludgeon, not a bad instrument for furnishing the long wide gabri, or wallet, which loads his broad back. If the costume be remarkable, the wearer in point of countenance and demeanour, is a real curiosity. I never saw even amongst the horrid looking devotees of India, a face in which the man, the baboon, and the fiend, are so fearfully and so wonderfully blended together. As for the individual's manners, you will soon see enough of them.

He is aware that we are approaching: though he neither moves from his seat, nor opens his half closed eyes, he shows consciousness by stringing his scapulary over his wrist, and by drawing forth the horn of a wild goat through which he begins to too-too with lugubrious perseverance. He then stretches out his cup, expecting alms.

"Give to me, men, give to me, d'ye hear me?"

I will make him show off his politeness.

"Take this bounty, O Fakir!—a rupee—and let us have the benefit of thy prayers in return for it!"

The fellow receives the coin in his gourd, rises slowly from the ground, and retreats a step or two, keeping his fiery red eyes shifting between the present and our countenances. He is direly offended.

"Bounty!—May Allah preserve you (with desperate irony). Bounty! it is my right—my due—my daily bread—my God's gift, not yours! One rupee; O, ye brothers of Hatim!*—one rupee! Time was when men gave me a thousand. You wear Moslem garments—ye crows dressed in parrot's feathers!—Corpses and eaters of corpses!—whose faces are blacker than yours? There, go your ways. A bad road and a curse to you."

When visiting holy places, Mr. Bull, I always make up my mind to eat dirt. We might order our servants, who, in spite of the sanctity of Kalandarhood, look eagerly for the job, to instruct the fellow in the *bienséances*. But he would certainly use his staff; the dagger might then appear, and the consequence

* Hatim the Arab chief had a brother, who attempting and failing to imitate his generosity, has succeeded in making himself celebrated for illiberality.

would be a serious fray. It will be better to leave him a Roland for his Oliver, and to get through our pilgrimage as quickly as possible.

"Abubekr, Omar, and Usman be — confounded! Go thy ways, O follower of an infamous patron saint!"*

We leave him speechless with fury.

"O, my father! O, my father!" cries a lady of flaunty dress and jaunty demeanour, standing and staring at us as if she had been a promenader of Fleet Street. "What men are these? Are ye going to pass through Sehwan, fellows, without engaging me for a nautch? Infidel Franks! Ye blights upon the land! *You* ruling instead of Ameers—ye locusts!"

That mouth it will be impossible to close. Our only way to save our ears from the "cudgel of her tongue," is to get beyond its range as speedily as we can. I will not, however, neglect to leave behind a few such "counter-checks quarrelsome" as "Thy locks be shaved!—dame of all the dogs!" "May thy nose drop off, eater of the pig!"—"May the jackass that carries thee (*i. e.* in procession through the

* It is a deadly insult to abuse a man's "pir" (patron saint, or spiritual guide).

basan) be a big ass !"—"May sweepers deposit their burdens upon thy corpse, O widow woman!"—"O thy mother, O thy sister, female fiend!"

We leave the lady blowing off her wrath in a long howl, varied and modulated by patting the palm of her hand against the circular orifice formed by her lips—the Indian and Scindian way of doing what Mrs. B. would effect by springing a rattle, or shrieks of "murder"—raising the neighbourhood.

Everything in this place seems to hate us. Even the pet tiger, as he catches sight of our white faces, shakes off the purring little cats who amuse themselves with walking over his broad flanks, springs up, glaring at us with blood-thirsty eyes, and ears viciously flattened upon his back, and walks round his cage as fast as his feet, lamed by the retractile claws growing into the flesh, allow him. The ferocious beast obtains almost religious honours from the superstitious populace who, by some curious mental process, connect him with Ali,* their favourite hero. His cage door is scarcely fastened, and his refectory is most bountifully supplied. When he amuses himself with tearing off the arm that offers him food, all predict good

* One of Ali's titles being "The Victorious *Lion* of the Lord."

luck and high honour in this world and the next to the maimed one. He has lately been playing the trick. If you wish to irritate the crowd around his box, you have only to propose, with a serious face, what you think the savage brute deserves —shooting him.

* * * *

This is the honoured tomb of Usmani Merwandi, popularly called the Kalandar—vagrantsaint—Lall Shahbaz, or the Red Falcon of Merwand, his natal province. He owes his curious ecclesiastical titles solely to his own exertions. Having once sat for a whole year in an iron pot placed upon a boiling fire, to imitate Ibrahim,* his skin, when he issued from the place of trial, had, as might be expected, exchanged the pallor of sanctity for a deep rubicund hue. On another occasion he assumed a winged form to rescue a brother in Allah from the stake upon which an infidel king had exalted his venerable form. Hence he is called Lall Shahbaz, a name that at once embodies the heads of his exploits, and distinguishes him from his fellows—scarlet hawks being novelties in the

* Abraham being unjustly accused of impiety by his father, Azar the idol maker, was thrown by the wicked Nimrod into a fiery furnace, which became a bed of roses for his reception. So writes Moslem Writ.

animal creation. Heedless of this nonsense, you, Mr. Bull, will probably judge him kindly when you hear that according to history he was a quiet, harmless old gentleman, who, very like many a fellow of Christ Church and Trinity College, preferred single blessedness, became highly moral, as he advanced in years, and died, leaving behind him a high reputation as a grammarian, a logician, a philologist, and a divine. There are points of difference in the comparison: the Kalandar I fear was "low church" and probably never drank crusty old port—however!

The Mausoleum, one of the seven wonders of the Scindian world, for magnitude as well as magnificence, would be a third-rate building in any semi-civilised part of India. In order to view the shrine, we must deposit our slippers at the threshold: then perhaps the jingling of a few rupees in our pockets may induce the surly scowling crowd to open a ready way. *En passant*, remark if you please the remains of splendour on the doors: anciently they were plates of massive silver, with gold locks, padlocks, and hinges; now wood is more extensively used. The interior is dark, dingy, and insufferably close, filled in equal proportions with animal caloric, the fumes of rancid incense, and the heavy smoke of long-wicked oil lamps. Under the dome is the holy place covered with a large satin pall, and hung over with a variety of silken, velvet, brocade and tinsel articles, shaped like little hearts—you may see them in southern Europe—or your old grandmother's pincushion. The walls, dimly illumined by a ray of light from door or lamp, are hung round with votive offerings of every description: the darkness and the dirt with which antiquity has overspread them, conceal them from our eyes profane.

The tomb is surrounded by devotees of all sexes and ages in crowds. Many people travel from Hyderabad — a hundred miles — and more distant places, for the mundane and post-mundane benefits secured by the pilgrimage. Some are sitting here supplicating his saintship to intercede for them with Allah, bribing him with promised dainties and rich clothes, which, though he wants not, his successors do. That hopeless cripple wishes to take up his bed and walk; the blind beggar is determined to see again; the pensive old person with the long beard is praying for the ruin of a favourite enemy, and the wrinkled old lady for a son and heir. A few grateful hearts are only thanking the holy corpse for past benefits, and a great many in whom the old Adam is, I fear, very strong, are savouring in anticipation the sweets of *indulgenza plenaria*—license to sin *ad libitum*. The men in the large turbans, with stolid faces, are the mullahs, or priests; the half-clad attendants are the mujawirs, whose duty it is to sweep the floor and trim the lamps; the stout ruffian with the shaven head, beard, eyebrows, and moustaches, is a promising young mendicant, who has just been affiliated to the order; and the two fellows sitting at the doors in the airy costume now familiar to your eye, and wrangling with every one, male or female, about the nature of his or her offering, are murshids, or masters in the mystic brotherhood of beggary. The latter, however, despite their dignity, do not always have their own way. Sometimes a swaggering Beloch, or a formidable-tongued Scindian dame will press in with no other present but a promise, and take place amongst the throng, seated, bowing and prostrating, groaning, mumbling, ejaculating, blessing and cursing one another round the sepulchre. If we stay here half an hour we are sure to see a kind of fight—if at least rending of garments and hauling of hair deserve that honoured name—between the collectors of church money and the votaries of an unexpensive religion, an unpaid worship.

You smile at these ridiculous altercations, Mr. Bull. So do I, with *dolce memoria* of having been similarly situated years ago—opposed at the threshold of an English chapel in one of our smaller continental settlements, by an Italian servant, who, having scant faith in credit, and possibly recollecting his own proverb, "*passato il pericolo, gabbato il santo,*" resisted my attempts to take a seat as sturdily as that fakir does, and triumphant, sent me home to fetch the forgotten "*pavolo*" for the *Signor Padre.*

It is the time of evening prayers, as we learn by the discordant clamours of half a dozen large brass kettle-drums in the Naubat khaneh* hard by: this oriental Ave Maria only tells me that 'tis the hour for a greater crowd to assemble, bringing with it more noise, more anger, more perspiration. So, if you please, we will leave our offering and a few civil words with the old khalifeh,† who, in compliment to

* A Persian term for the room in which the kettle-drums are placed and performed upon.

† The worthy upon whom the prophetic or saintly mantle falls.

our dresses, has attended personally to do the honours of his raree-show, and depart.

The centre of Sehwan attraction lies within a few minutes' walk. It is a large flat mound, based upon a rock, rising abruptly from the plain, supported by the cohesiveness of its clay, and in some places flanked by the remnants of good old brick walls, bastions, and circular towers, round which gnarled peepuls and knotty shrubs of huge growth, have coiled their snake-like roots.

Mounting the side of the mound by a natural breach in it, and striking into one of the many foot-paths that ramify over it, we find the surface cut up by wind and rain, rent by yawning sun-cracks, and occasionally mined by the seekers of gold, silver, and ready-made material for building. A glimpse from the brink of one of these cavities shows that the brickwork runs down almost to the level of the road that girds the clay hill, and the excavators will inform us that when they first opened the ground they discovered and destroyed large arches.

This is one of the many remains of what are ridiculously termed "Alexander's camp" by the Anglo-Scindian antiquary. Macedonia's great man, observe,

Mr. Bull, holds in this country the architectural office assigned by you and your brethren to the Devil and Julius Cæsar in the West. That is to say, whenever a tourist of inquiring mind is shown a ruin about which that great authority, the "oldest inhabitant," knows nothing, or will not know anything, he considers himself justified in at once deciding it to be an "Alexander's camp."

This Sehwan mound cannot be of Grecian origin, I humbly opine, for two reasons. The arches are Asiatic, and the broken bits of man's handiwork found scattered about in its entrails are oriental. If we are to believe the chronicles, it was a Hindoo castle built to command a favourite ford of the Indus: in the lapse of years, as it was ruined and ruined over again, the site rose above the level of the plain, till at last it became conspicuous, and, catching the archæologist's eye, it received from his ready hand the honours of an illustrious origin.

The natives of Scinde, excepting only the few readers of Persian poetry and history, had never heard of "Sikandar Shah"* when we first entered the country. Now they bid fair to become almost as

* King Alexander.

minute and clever in pointing out the different stages of his progress through the land as our *savans* have proved themselves. So the Affghans, after one short year's study of the British *gobemouche*, taught themselves to imitate the rare Bactrian coins with a skill, which, considering all their deficiences of means, entitles them, I opine, to rank high in the scale of ingenious rascality.

There are no traditions of consequence connected with this old fort. The people as usual believed the gloomy deserted place to be haunted, especially by night, and it was some time before the deputy-collector, who erected a bungalow, with *naïve* nationality, upon the summit, could persuade his Scindian servants that they could sleep in it without imminent peril of being eaten. Him they knew to be safe. The Franks are all magicians: any real Oriental will inform you, that the reason why we never see their legions of goblins is simply that we are the "fathers of devils"—that is to say fiercer fiends than the general run of fiery creatures.* When a lady in Persia wishes to cast abomination between her husband and a pretty little rival wife, she secretly

* Fiends, say the Moslems, are made of fire, as man is of earth.

rubs a bit of pork upon the latter's dress; and the good Moslem forthwith conceives a violent loathing for the object of his love. What think you, Mr. Bull, must be expected from a people who eat grilled bacon for breakfast, and at times dine off a sucking pig?

CHAPTER XXIV.

LAKE MANCHAR.—LARKHANA THE PRETTY, AND MAHTAB, THE DONNA OF LARKHANA.

Open the map of Scinde, sir, and listen to me.

A little north of Larkhana, on the right bank of the Indus, you see a streaky line marked Narrah R. that is to say, the Snake River—a Scinde Serpentine. It falls into an oval which stands for a lake—Manchar—flows through it, and issues from the southern extremity under a fresh name, the Aral. These—the Narrah and the Aral—form a semicircle of about sixty miles from point to point; they are probably artificial: their tortuous course presents the appearance of man's rather than Nature's doings. The country is so level that, when the Indus rises, the water flows up the Aral, and *vice versâ*, when the main stream falls.

Two days' journey* along the Aral from Sehwan before we reach the lake.

* * * *

At this season of the year you will admire Mahar Manchar—Great Manchar, as the people are fond of calling it—especially after the arid scenes of the Mimosa Bank and the Lukkee Hills. A sheet of crystalline blue, waved with the tiniest ripple that zephyr ever ruffled up, broken by little flat capes and green headlands, and pigmy brown cliffs, spreads far to the west, there indistinctly limited by a long broad curtain of yellow hill. Down the centre of its length runs a line of deep channel, amethyst-coloured, except where the fisher's canoe glides, whitening the surface of the wave: all around, the lovely Lotus—one understands them that gave her for gods and goddesses to handle—raises her pearly head, and veils with her emerald cloak the pellucid nakedness of the shallower streams. The banks are forested with sedge and reeds, thick and shaggy as old Proteus' drying locks; and high above the rank thicket towers the knotted kano, with its tall columnar stalk

* From Sehwan to Bazar, ten; from Bazar to Drabri, a fishing village on Lake Manchar, eleven miles.

and light feathery top, gracefully bending and bowing to the breeze.

Nor is the prospect wanting in "figures"—a *sine quâ non*, methinks, in any but an Arctic or a Central African view. In some parts the water is almost concealed from sight by the multitude of wild birds, feeding and floating, swimming and trimming their plumage upon the crystal flood. There is the Brahminee duck, with his brilliant hues; the king curlew, with his black coat and scarlet cap; the flamingo, rosy and snowy white; the fawn-coloured pelican, little smaller than an ostrich; the tall bittern, with his yellow ruff; and, queen amongst these nobles, the graceful saras,* clad in delicate blue, with a head of brilliant crimson, shading off with the sweetest gradations of red and pink down her long taper neck. Mingling with the patriarchs of the air, the commonalty — mallards and cormorants, snipes and snippets, dabchicks and ducks, of different descriptions—pursue their several avocations. Above us, the elegant tern wheels in butterfly-like flight; and the little kingfisher, now poised aloft, twittering his sharp clear note with his beak resting on his breast, now

* A large kind of stork.

flashing through the sunbeam like a handful of falling gems, as he tries his fortune in the depths below, claims our recognition as an old acquaintance.

The human is almost as abundant as the lower animal population of Maha Manchar. In some spots the scene viewed from afar reminds you of Chinese voyages and travels. At this moment we see at least a hundred little black boats, moored against the reedy banks, or entangled in the foliage of the lake, or pushing out into the main stream, where the fisherman may cast his nets, fearless of tough stalk and tangled root.

The Mohana or Scinde fishermen are, to judge from their swarthy skins and Indian features, directly descended from the aboriginal Hindoos, converted to Islam. The change has not hitherto raised them high above heathenism: they still pay a kind of religious respect to the element—their nurse: they never enter the water without praying it, by a salaam, not to be their grave just yet; and their rice offerings and hymns addressed to the river god savour rankly of old idolatry. They are an athletic, laborious, merry-hearted, debauched, and thoroughly demoralised set of half-savages. Women as well as men all seem to be in a state of perpetual motion—whether the result of a fish diet or not, I leave you, Mr. Bull, to determine: certainly, the contrast their activity offers to the general torpidity of Scindianism, deserves a little philosophico-physiological consideration. Sturdy fishwives are seen tugging at the oar, or paddling at the stern, whilst the spouse busily plies the net: the elder children, in nature's habiliment, dabble about like water-fowl, and the Benjamin of the family lies consoling himself, sucking his thumb, in a cot of network, that dangles high in the air between the mast and the rigging of the little craft. They eat, drink, smoke, and sleep on board their vessels, these amphibious animals, and never quit them except to cure their prey, to dry it upon the banks, and to sell it or exchange it at the nearest market village for the necessaries of life. They are equally celebrated for depravity and devotion; seldom marry till, orientally speaking, old; and scrupulously spend every farthing they can secrete from the mullah, in bhang, opium, and spirituous liquors. Their families are remarkably large: in addition to the general activity of their bodies, their tongues—especially those of the ladies—seem gifted with uncommon nimbleness, and the proceeds translated into our vernacular would be a novel and valuable addition to the vocabulary of Billingsgate. Perhaps these also are the effects of a fish diet. Withal, the Mohanas are a merry light-hearted race, except when cold, or when recovering from intoxication: they enjoy a rude jest—only it must be rude—almost as much as a glass of liquor, and never seem to quarrel with fate, except when an embryo fisherman slips overboard and exchanges its cradle for a watery grave. Little can be said in favour of their appearance; their skins are burned to a reddish-black by the searing wind and scorching sun; their features fearfully resemble the developist's First Father; and their dress consists of two dirty cloths, one wound round the head, the other tightly wrapped about the loins. Some of the youngest damsels are pretty; occasionally one sees a face which may be pronounced handsome, but a hard life, in every sense of the word, induces middle age at twenty; and Macbeth never saw such hags as you do in the old Mohani.

We view Manchar in its very best hour. During the summer it is the most execrable place in Scinde;

and popular indignation has expressed itself in a proverb, the purport of which is, that while this exists, no other Pandemonium is necessary. As the heat increases, the almost stagnant water, and the fat weeds which spring from the black slime bottom, send forth swarms of musquitos and sand-flies, gnats and dragon-flies, midges and common flies, whilst Quartana, Tertiana, and all their unholy sisterhood, hover like harpies on the devoted shore. At times, too, the lake, now so placid, chafes itself into all the fury of Geneva or the Mediterranean. A blast of wind comes howling over and stirring up the waters which rise to the summons of the storm-fiend, as if some kindred devil were immured in them. Then woe to you, voyager! There are no waves to ride over, nothing but a broken surface of short chopping sea, black below, foaming above, every billow unconnected with its neighbour, and each one perfectly capable of swamping your little boat. If caught in one of these hurricanes you have only to be prepared for the worst—drowning in luke-warm water. Mooring, from the nature of the banks, is impossible. You must give your craft her head; allow her to run away with you wherever she pleases; and congratulate yourself, indeed, upon your good luck, if, when "spilt" into a field of hedge-like sedges, you do not sink into the mud deeper than the neck, before the storm subsides, and some fisher's canoe comes off to your rescue.

* * * *

To Larkhana, eight stages.*

We have now quitted Wicholo, and are within the bounds of Siro—Northern Scinde. The Egyptian fertility of the soil commences: here you may calculate, Mr. Bull, what our Unhappy Valley is capable of becoming worth. The bed of the river is higher and nearer the surface of the country than it is in the lower provinces; the canals are better excavated, and the result is that water is more easily procurable. Instead of the dirty, ragged clumps of huts which you were accustomed to see, neat and comfortable little hamlets, surrounded by groves of date, jujube, and neem trees, meet the eye in all directions. The grazing land is black and white with buffalos, cows, and goats; crops begin to gladden the fields: we hear the music of the Persian wheels from the shafts and tunnels dug in the river and canal banks,

* Namely, Chenni, ten miles; Johi, fourteen; Phulajee, fifteen; Gharra, thirteen; Mehr, eighteen; Nasirabad, seventeen; Khairpur, thirteen; and Larkhana, eleven.

and the loud shouts of the corn-keepers, slinging away at the hungry birds from their little raised platforms, sound human, busy, energetic. The cultivators are no longer lean with hunger, pallid with enlarged spleen, half clad, reckless and indolent with poverty. Every man walks as if he had an object: he has a burly waist, and he looks at us almost benignantly. As we ride through the hamlets, peering curiously, and like Englishmen over the walls of the court-yard, and into the doors of the houses, comely olive-coloured female ovals, with immense black eyes, and the whitest possible teeth, are protruded to catch sight of the strangers, and these same, instead of being withdrawn with a half convulsive jerk, are, pleasant to relate, allowed to remain for the pleasure of mutual inspection. Here and there, where the settlement is a very flourishing one, we may indulge ourselves in an amiable bow, the effect of which will be an amused smile instead of an angry mutter at the "brass" of the European face under the Asiatic turban.

Larkhana is in the centre of Scindia Felix—the summer-house of the garden about it. The town is pleasantly situated upon the bank of a large canal, girt by groves of spreading trees, which checker with shade the holcus and wheat fields. It contains the usual stuff of a Scindian town, but *tout en beau.* The mosques are larger, the tanks are better built, the big houses are more numerous, and the small houses are less squalid than our old models. There is an extensive bazaar, containing several hundred shops, which strikes us with a sense of splendour; and at one end of the town rises a kind of citadel, called Fort Fitzgerald, from the gallant officer who superintended its erection, impressing us with ideas of security. Larkhana is a place of some commerce. It is known for its manufactures of coarse cloth, and, being upon the high-road between Kurrachee and Shikarpur, it is the favourite station with caravans and travelling merchants. This is probably the reason why it is celebrated for anything but morality. The inhabitants are a dissolute race, fond of intoxication, dancing, and other debauchery, and idle, because the necessaries are so cheap that there is no need of working hard to live. The number of fair Corinthians in the place has given it a proverbial bad name in the mouths of moral-minded Scindians.

I promised you a nautch, Mr. Bull, and Hari

Chand has secured the services of a celebrated lady of pretty name, Mahtab—the "Moonbeam:" here she comes with her sisters, each sitting in her own kajawah*—altogether a train of nine camels.

Mahtab, the Donna of Larkhana, is quietly beautiful as her namesake. The exact setting of every feature in that perfect oval of hers gives her as many lovely faces as there are varying positions for that one. The gloss of youth is on her hair and marble-like transparent skin—mouth, eyebrows, eyelashes, all look new, unused, fresh as the day they were finished by the hand of Nature. The expression of her countenance is strange in one so admirable and so admired: it is settled melancholy, as if the owner had been a victim to some *grande passion*—which, by the by, is not the case. You cannot help every now and then wishing that a smile, or a frown, or a sneer would rumple those finished lips, that tall, calm brow—that she would appear somewhat more human, less like a statue in a moonlit walk.

Your eyes, weary with the beauties of her face, shift to her figure, where, if perfection ever was, there

* A kind of camel litter; a pair of gigantic ladle-shaped panniers, in which Scindian ladies stow themselves away.

you discover it. Your glance slowly takes in a throat, to which "tower of ivory," "gazelle's neck," and all that kind of thing, would be studied insults: thence it shifts lingeringly to a line of shoulder, where, if it could, it would stay; but on it must go, to understand what a bust is, and to see what a woman's waist might be—not, as you shudderingly recollect, what it is so often made to be—thence—

But stop, Mr. Bull. At this rate you will be falling in love with the Moonbeam:—I tremble to think of the spirit in which your lapse would be received by the bonneted, well curled, be-mantled, straight-laced, be-petticoated partner of your bosom. I would almost engage you to say nothing of the scene when you return home: it would grieve me even to dream of "minx" and "savage" in connection with yonder masterpiece of prettiness.

A sigh at the idea, and we will give a signal for the start.

The musicians, one pipe, one guitar, and two kettledrums, sit down heavily upon rugs in a corner of the tent: opposite them are the ladies, who, with the exception of Mahtab—bless her instinct!—have hung gold in every bit of attainable cartilage, and converted themselves into bales of brocade and satin elaborately mixed. Their toilette, I need scarcely remark, is the acme of *la mode:* they can scarcely stand on their slippers, the tightness of their shalwars round their ancles impedes the lower circulation, and their hair is strained off their foreheads so tightly as almost to pull their features out of place. There are swords, daggers, and shields in the party, and, more dangerous still, sundry flasks and phials containing a colourless liquid, which I am told is water, which I believe to be something stronger.

The nautch commences with a *pas seul:* the Moonbeam is going to engross every eye. You perhaps expect one of those grievous and laborious displays of agility, to which Europe has limited professional dancing. Oh, no! An *entrechat* in these regions would shave a girl's head, a *pas de Zephyre* bleed her, and half-a-dozen *petits battements* consign her to a dark inner room without windows and with bare walls. Mahtab floats forward so softly that trace of exertion is imperceptible: slowly waving her white arms, she unexpectedly stands close to you, then turning with a *pirouette*—it has no other name, but its nature is widely different from the whirligig rotations of a Taglioni—she sinks back, retires and stands motionless as wax-work, and then again all *da capo*, with the beautiful sameness that becomes her face and figure. The guitar is in the seventh heaven of ecstacy, the pipe is dying away with delight, and the kettledrums threaten to annhilate their instruments. The lady's sisters or rather sisterhood are too completely under the spell even to feel envious, and you, Mr. Bull, are inclined to vociferate, as is your wont, "*Brav-o!*"

There is nothing particularly interesting or exciting in the *pas de deux*, and the other trifles in which Mahtab's companions display themselves, whilst the beauty sits motionlessly reposing. You feel that there is something in her look which spurns rather than courts ardent eyes, and you are disposed to yawn after a minute's inspection of the troop, and to contort your countenance when you fix your ear upon the Chinese melody of the music. The musicians may amuse you for a moment. They are all *en train* towards that happy state aptly described by the merry, scandalous monarch, as levelling all artificial distinctions between sovereign and subject. They drink well but not wisely: those tossings of the head intended to beat time, those merciless rubbings of stubby beard and wild mustachio, purporting excitement, and those bendings of the body that remind you of the cockswain in a rowing match, all tend towards "under the table," were there such an article of furniture in the tent.

Now for the ballet, or melodrama, the favourite piece of the evening. The ladies all equip themselves in manly and martial dresses—all, except the "Donna," whom dignity forbids.

En passant, I may remark that this way of confusing the sexes, though adverse to high histrionic effect, is by no means so utterly disenchanting as that for which our amateur Anglo-Indian theatres are remarkable. A pretty girl's face under a man's helmet, and a delicate female arm supporting a rhinoceros skin targe are, to say the least, endurable. Not so soft Juliet, when a monster of a horse artilleryman, six feet, by three across the shoulders, with fiery whiskers and a voice like the lowing of distant kine; or dear Desdemona represented by a pale, weasen-faced, cock-nosed, intensely ugly, and broken-voiced little lad, in the first state of change from school-boy to "officer and gentleman."

The piece is a species of comedy, in which a youthful, beautiful, and coquettish wife, an old and irate husband, and a young and ardent lover—all lustily dancing—represent sundry scenes of probable occurrence in Eastern domestic life. Either in consequence of the plot's engrossing interest, or the contents of those flasks, there is much palpable exaggeration in the development of "character"—never was old husband so thoroughly irate as this one, never young lover so ardent, never pretty wife such an *outrée* coquette. And alas for the poetical justice and the morality of the muse in Scinde! The rightful owner of the coveted goods at length falls to the ground, pierced by twenty deadly wounds, whilst the breaker of ever so many commandments, after carefully securing his fallen foe's sword, best dagger, and new turban, walks off with the "bone of contention" as quietly as if it had been his own rightful "rib." And, again, alas for the degradation of the professionals in the valley of the Indus! one of the kettle-drums has with considerable difficulty been removed by two of our Affghan servants, the pipe is going fast, and extraneous aid is necessary to the drooping form of Nur Jan, the Moonbeam's youngest and prettiest sister. We ought not to have admitted those flasks.

* * * *

Larkhana is celebrated for another kind of nautch, which I would willingly show you, were it not haunting as a good ghost story or a bad novel.

Conceive, if you can, the unholy spectacle of two reverend-looking grey-beards, with stern, severe, classical features, large limbs, and serene, majestic deportment, dancing opposite each other dressed in women's attire; the flimsiest too, with light veils on their heads, and little bells jingling from their ankles, ogling, smirking, and displaying the juvenile playfulness of

"— limmer lads and little lassies!"

CHAPTER XXV.

THE PICTURESQUE "SUKKUR, BUKKUR, ROHRI."

A trio of words not unknown to modern Indian fame. When the Bengal seapoy wished to address his comrade with a friendly and polite curse, he would jocosely say,

Are bhai! Sukkur, Bukkur, Rohriko jao!

Which—"Go to Sukkur, Bukkur, Rohri, my brother"—thus became the equivalent for an expression immensely popular amongst British soldiers and sailors.

At this season of the year—early February—Sukkur will surprise you by its delightful climate. The mornings and evenings are as cool as they would be in Tuscany; there is a tonic draught in the pure light air, and the breeze out of the sun is bracing as well as sweet. This state of things will last at least twenty days longer, but then.— In fact, without this preparation against the summer heat, the capital of Upper Scinde would be uninhabitable to the western man.

* * * *

Here we stand, after four days of marching,* at the Belvidere of Sukkur. I have not erred, you see, in characterising it as the "picturesque." Before us, in the distance, the broad tranquil Indus, flowing slowly from the west to east, suddenly sweeps round towards the south, and dashing through two rocky beds narrowed to eight hundred yards, descends, like the preliminary to a cataract, in the direction where we stand. On the right is the huge irregular mass of mud walls that compose Rohri, with its conspicuous mosque overhanging the stream, and its beautiful date and garden grounds behind. On the rocky islets which split the Indus rise the crumbling walls of Bukkur, and the domed fane of Khwajah Khizr,† half concealed by a screen of dark green trees. On the left are the fortified heights and the precipitous banks, crowned by turrets and habita-

* Larkhana to Naya Dera thirteen miles; Madadji, fourteen; Jarli, seventeen; Sukkur, fifteen.

† A popular Moslem saint who was, it is said, a servant of Moses, a great prophet, Phineas, Elijah, and the River Indus, and is a kind of wandering Jew who drank the water of immortality, never dies, and becomes all kinds of people.

tions that bear the name of Sukkur;* whilst the foreground is occupied by a large bazaar full of natives, sufficiently hidden by the tall colonnade and the tufted tops of giant palms.

Particularly attractive is this view when seen at the morning hour. The sun slowly tops "Fort Victoria on the Indus,"* and dashes with crimson the opposite part of the elsewhere azure stream: the depths of the air sparkle with blue; light mists soar from the lowlands, giving a charm of indistinctness to the distant prospect; and near us the contrast between the features that stand out in the horizontal beams and those about which the purple shade of dawn still lingers, is as striking as any amateur of the picturesque could desire.

With one glance you perceive, Mr. Bull, how this bit of ground came to be so thickly built over. In ancient days, when the Indus—say geographers—washed round the entire shoulder of the Sukkur Hills, it was, you may be sure, bleak and barren enough. Presently † the stream shifted its

* The new name of Bukkur, very seldom used.

† This channel could not have existed in Alexander's day without attracting the attention of his historians. The Moslems connect the change, by tradition, with a time subsequent to their conquests in Scinde.

course to the present channel, "cutting away the looser strata of the limestone ridge, and leaving the harder masses, one of which forms the island, and others the hills on the Sukkur side of the river. Bukkur, with the moat which nature thus threw round it, and the least assistance of the mason's art, in days when howitzers and mines were unknown, must have been a kind of inland Gibraltar. It was considered for ages the key of Scinde. Hemmed in, and at times cut off from communication with the land, the settlement was doubtless more important than comfortable or convenient, for which reason the towns of Rohri and Sukkur sprang up on either side of it.

I will do Cicerone upon them, beginning with Rohri, the elder.

Rohri, like most places in saint-bearing Scinde, is a sacred spot. The traditions of the country romance its origin as follows. A shepherd, who used to feed his flocks in these parts, observed every night a dazzling luminous appearance, which at first he supposed to be some caravan's watch-fire. The phenomenon, however, continuing regularly, at last aroused his curiosity: he despatched his wife to ascertain what it might be. The good woman, after many fruitless endeavours to approach the flame, which danced away from her, and vanished in a preternatural manner, went back to her husband, and told him all the strange facts she had witnessed. He, in his turn, attempted to near the light, and, like his wife, failed to do so. What remained for him to conclude but that the appearance was a miraculous one, and that it was sent to him to be, what my Scotch Major used to call a "solemn warning?" As Scindians, favoured with visions from the dark world generally appear to do, the shepherd threw aside all the pomps and vanities of this, his wife included, and erecting a takiyah or fakir's seat, became a beggar and a man of Allah. Rohri, therefore, in all probability, owes its origin to a " Will o' the wisp,"—quite as good an ancestor methinks as a sliced bull's hide, or a dozen of vultures — setting aside the minor consideration that these historical vultures were, one may suspect, real carrion crows.

In the sixteenth century of our era a holy native of Istambol, or Constantinople, emigrated—for what reason it is not said—to Scinde. Finding Rohri a flourishing place, rich in temporalities as well as in spiritual gifts, he deposited, in the Jamma Masjid, or the town Cathedral,* the Mui Mubarik, or Holy Hair,—a pile and a half from the prophet's venerable beard. The relic stood its trial triumphantly as any vial of Virgin's milk or cuttings of St. Peter's toe-nails, and performed such incontestable supernaturalities, that Scepticism, strange to say, was at a nonplus, whilst Faith flocked from all four quarters of the Moslem world, to perform pilgrimage and merit well from heaven. The hair throve, inclosed in a golden tube, studded with rubies and precious stones; pious keepers, called mujawirs, took charge of it, and also throve, so did the mosque, and so, in consequence, did universal Rohri. Thus, the town owed its elevation to a hair and a half—a circumstance at which the learned archæo-historiographer will by no means turn up his nose.

But holiness—in this one respect how obedient to the law of changes which govern things profane!—hath her day, and impious Time kicks over, with equal foot, the mosque, the palace, and the Ryot's cot. Rohri is still a sacred place, but its sanctity is

* This building, however, as we are informed by an inscription, was erected in the Emperor Akhbar's time, about A. D. 1575.

worn out, decrepit, broken down with years. The town is almost in ruins; its old fortifications are even with the ground, and its houses appear only temporarily elevated above the same level. The two scourges of the East, the priest and the chief, have been busy at undermining its very foundations: the former insisted not only upon devouring the fat of the land; he also demanded, and obtained, the largest and most expensive establishments, colleges, and houses devoted to supplying him with successors. The latter, who had his seat at Khairpur, a neighbouring town, plundered it of all the church left unplundered. Rohri may now, Mr. John Bull, be likened, in worldly matters, to an aged bankrupt who has passed triumphantly through the court,—obscurely secure and permanently ruined.

Bukkur, the next of the trio, is perched, as you have seen, upon a rock, some thirty feet above the level of the Indus, well commanded by both banks. It came into our hands by a peculiar effect of diplomatic head work. In a treaty, concluded with the late Talpur Ameers, or Lords, of Khairpur, a significant clause had been introduced by those crafty barbarians, stipulating that the gentlemen with white faces should not appropriate to themselves "any of the forts *on either side the Indus.*" Whereupon, the British Talleyrand astutely remarking that "it is curious how cunning people outwit themselves," laid violent hands upon Bukkur, considering it unclaimed ground *in* (not *on*) the river. So that, in due course of time, the "British ensign was," as we are informed, "planted on this important fortress." It received a Christian name on the occasion of its conversion, and was highly praised by its new possessors, probably on the principle that we always think better of stolen fruit.

Bukkur now consists of a dilapidated baked-brick wall, which looks as if you might breach it with a pocket pistol, and a *terre pleine*, partly a bare surface, partly covered with stumps of masonry. It is still useful to the ordnance department as a store-house, and in my day, Mr. Bull, was employed by the military authorities as a retirement to which subalterns were liable to be sent, on pretext of guard, out of harm's way—secure from the dissipation of Sukkur and the depravity of Shikarpur. Tho two well wooded little islands near Bukkur, are remarkable for their domes, their sanctity, and the circumstance that the fishes* always retire from, even as they approach them, with rigid court ceremonial.

Sukkur, when we visited it, had almost lost vitality, —one thousand inhabitants were all that remained to it. The first restorative administered to its constitution was the establishment of a military cantonment. Barracks were erected for Europeans, lines for Asiatic soldiery. As all the crests of the little hills around had been built over with the mausolea of dead venerables, the tombs were seized upon and converted into bungalows, by the officers, with such zeal, that even Masum's Minaret †—the Monument of Sukkur—was in imminent danger of being converted into a "Griffin Hall." Then arose bazaars, shops in multitudes, and Parsee stores, full of ham, pickles, pale ale, soda-water, curaçoa, and other necessaries. The Indus Flotilla was ordered to fix its head quarters here. In a word, Sukkur became a flourishing place. Its prosperity was not of a permanent de-

* Certainly the Pullah fish is rarely, if ever, caught above the island of Bukkur—it cannot swim against such a stream.

† A tower ninety or a hundred feet high, erected over the tomb of Mohammed Masum of Bukkur; a wealthy and powerful Sayyid in the days of Akhbar the Great. The building is ascended by a winding stone stair; it commands a fine panoramic view of the country, and I believe I am justified in stating that a man once precipitated himself from its summit.

scription, principally, I believe, because no earthly power could keep fifty out of a hundred soldiers alive in it one year round. The experiment, of course, was tried and retried,—some over-scrupulous folks dclared it was over-tried—but such perseverance only proved that the unhappy Bill Smiths, Ned Greens, and Jack Browns—100*l.* a head is said to be the price of them—died in numbers ruinous to the state.

Old Sukkur has a fort kept in such order, that the morning and midday guns cannot be fired from the rampart for fear of accidents. I will spare you the trouble of lionising it. Besides the "monument," there is but one building in the town at all remarkable, a handsome mosque, domed, encrusted with variegated tiles, like those at Tattah, and provided with a snappish tiger like that at Sehwan. The principal houses, most of them reformed sepulchres, furnished with verandahs, and pierced for windows, are brick edifices perched upon little buttons of rock, sticking, here and there, a little out of the coat of dust, or dirt, which invests the inner plain. On the very banks of the river all is, comparatively speaking, happy in fertility and population—

half a mile away from it, nothing but the usual Scinde aspect of barrenness and desolation.

You see yon distant plain north of Rohri, where the naked cultivators are droning after their lazy cattle. I recollect a very different scene there—noise, bustle, and excitement. You may bear the recital of it, as hitherto, my dear Mr. Bull, you have not been so thoroughly Cobdenised or Elihu Burrited that you cannot feel

"The pomp and circumstance of glorious war;"

or can object to accompany Mrs. B. and the little Bulls—you grumble, of course, but that the English father always does on a "party of pleasure"—to a pigmy review of the household troops in the park.

Some time in 1846, the Sikhs, after kindly warning us of their hostile intentions so long and so often that we thoroughly believed them incapable of the action, crossed the Sutlej *en masse.* All Scinde, amongst other places, was in a turmoil—the cause, an order from her Governor for the assemblage of a large force on that plain, near Rohri.

It was a model army, complete in all points, —engineers, artillery, horse and foot, cavalry, regular and irregular, camel corps (a kind of four-footed light infantry), regiments of the line, white and black, and baggage corps—to prevent our luxuriousness. Under the guidance of the old soldier that was to head them, the 13,000 fighting men that composed the force would, I believe, have marched through the the heart of Central Asia as a cannon-ball into the curtain of a mud fort.

A most picturesque spectacle was the camp—a town of glittering white tents, laid out in mathematical streets and squares, thronged with gay uniforms and suburbed by guards and pickets, placed in the pleasure-gardens of Rohri, or on the natural quay that skirts the Indus. Orderlies were continually galloping up and down the lines, battalions manœuvring, and squadrons moving in all possible directions; the very river was covered with crazy boats, pontoons, and dhundhis * laden with stores. Every step was bustling, every face had a joyful *quid nunc* in it; the very camp-follower forgot to predict, as he always does, certain and disastrous consequences.

We were ordered to march upon Multan, then in possession of the Sikhs, by brigades of three regiments.

* A Scinde boat.—See Chapter XVIII.

A little after midnight, every morning, the dull drowsy silence of rest-time, broken only by the bay of a pariah dog, the monotonous tollings of the gong, and the periodical change of a guard, fled at that blithe sound of the trumpet, which one is sure to mistake for

> "Don't you hear the General say,
> 'Strike your tents, and march away?'"

A buzz and hum of many voices hails the first shrill blast; everything becomes conscious and active. The cavalry horses neigh; the infantry men chatter; the camels address angry remonstrance of loud roars to their loaders; the camp-followers, the servants, and the camp dogs,—we have little or none of the fair sex with us,—combine to make an uproar which would have made the Seven Sleepers start up in a twinkling.

The second bugle sounds!

Every tent is packed and loaded—everybody is so anxious to take Multan, that the blacks scarcely allow themselves the luxury of idling over a fire of bushes. Men tear their shins upon tent-pegs almost without a complaint, and jostle one another generally without cursing; the camel that bites at you seems to do it less from malice than as a bit of fun; so full is every one of laughter, that you cannot fall into a hole in the ground without exciting latent into loud haw-haws.

At the third trumpet, the long column winds away across the plain at the rate of four miles an hour through thick dust, over a heavy road, yet united in the firm determination not to feel sore heels or to limp with chafed toes. The arms are trailed; the European soldier produces his gruff *bon mot*, the native his rude chaunt and saturnalian jest; all listen to the Joe Miller of each section with irrepressible glee. We seldom arrive at the halting-ground before 7 or 8 A.M., a broiling hour in these regions, despite the powers of pedestrianism displayed by both colours, black and white. The road, cut up by the first columns, is almost knee-deep in dust, and the perpetual checks occasion numberless haltings; as no one abused the chills of the morning, so no one quarrels with the heat of the before-breakfast sun. Arrived at the ground, the soldier is too busy to discover, debate about, and represent, a beef or mutton grievance, and the seapoy too much excited to find fault with the attah,* or to swear rancidness against the clarified butter. Excited combativeness has by some means or other quickened the organ of benevolence.

Thirteen or fourteen days this scene lasted. We were almost within sight of "the key of the Punjaub,"† when suddenly a rumour came down upon us, chilling as the damp of a Scindian dawn. It altered the expression of every countenance: the white men looked black with surly disappointment, the black men white with volatile rage. Our Governor-General, of pacific memory, Sir H—— H——, had determined that the temple of Janus should be locked up, *coûte qui coûte*, once more. He had scotched the Sikh snake, and either forgetting, in his fury against war, that—

"The little viper becomes a big viper" (Persian proverb)—

—or possibly wishing another hand to do the executioner's dirty work, he left Multan† intact, uninjured, in the power of an active and wily foe. The policy was as strictly short-sighted as might be expected to proceed from a diplomatist with a hobby: it gave

* Flour which, kneaded into unleavened cakes, forms the Seapoy's "staff of life."

† Multan.

the enemy time to recover strength and courage, to assemble his men, to lavish his treasure,—our prize-money, Mr. Bull,—and to mature plans which eventually lost us many a valuable life, and cost us many a precious lac.

To conclude my episode of "much ado about nothing." We turned our heads southwards with heavy, very heavy hearts. Some regiments had the prospect of a 600 miles' march in April, before they reached summer quarters,—all the anticipation of a hot, sickly season in Scinde. Then did the scene change with a witness. Never was cold found so cold, heat so hot, roads so dusty, defiles so tiresome, attah so full of sand and grit, beef so bony and so bad; every footsore became an ulcer; every headache a stroke of the sun. There was little "malingering." The hospitals and doolies* were crowded with unpretending patients. Numbers died of fever, and many were half-blinded by ophthalmia, the offspring of silt-laden wind and torrid glare. To the eye of fancy, even the animal creation seemed to feel a share of our miseries; the horses hung down their heads in melancholy plight, scarcely caring to

* The dooly is a coarsely made palanquin, light and airy; it is generally used for carrying the sick, who cannot afford better means of conveyance.

snort away the clouds of pungent dust invading their nostrils; the camp-followers got drunk or committed felony in vain attempts to divert their minds; and the unfortunate camels, weighed down by hundred-weights of servants, who now recked little how soon they killed the beasts, roared and bellowed, stood and struggled regularly ten hours out of the twenty-four.

It was a dismal spectacle.

CHAPTER XXVI.

SHIKARPUR.—ITS CENTRAL ASIAN BAZAAR, AND ITS HINDOOS.

SHIKARPUR will be an interesting place to you, Mr. Bull, veteran admirer of commercial enterprise.

The city stands near the northern frontier, about twenty-five miles westward of Sukkur. Our march to it might be split into three or four stages; but, as we purpose a long halt at this last bourne of our pilgrimage through the Unhappy Valley, and as a "home" in the shape of a "mud edifice," duly hired and dusted, is awaiting us, I propose to push on at once.

This capital of merchants, bankers, and money-changers is an open town built upon a low alluvial plain, abounding as usual in fine dust and glitter. It is surrounded by gardens and trees, which impart a tinge of freshness to the view; anciently a mud wall, now broken by age into white mouldering fragments, and eight big, shady, eastern gates formed its rude defences. The suburbs are large and straggling; the streets narrow, crowded, and unclean. Unfortunately for the health of the place, water is found at twelve or thirteen feet below the surface of the ground, and the number of wells, each with its dependent pool of stagnant water, is ten times greater than required. There are no public buildings, except a few mosques, in the town, and the houses are for the most part composed of wood-work and sun-dried brick, with low verandahs, little glassless holes for light, and the other peculiarities of the oriental domicile. The bungalows of the civil and military officers attached to the station are outside the town.

Shikarpur possesses one curiosity—a Central Asian bazaar, the first thing of the kind we have seen. It is the main street of the town, a long, narrow, tall walled passage, darkened and guarded against the sun by mats laid upon the beams that connect house with house. Four, P.M., is the hour at which the Scindian merchant appears upon 'Change. Will you accompany me?

Here we have specimens of, at least, a dozen

nations under our eyes. The little Brahui, with his stalwart shoulders, flat face, and broad limbs, in camel's hair vest, stands gazing at the Halwai's * tempting store, with epicurean looks. A knot of Affghans are settling the prices of their camels. You can see what these men are by their tall, large forms, eager utterance, fiery eyes, and energetic gestures. Although not permitted to bear arms, their hands are deep in their waistbands, as if the wonted charay† were there waiting to be used. The wild Beloch, whose grizzled locks, blackened skin, and scarred cheek, tell mute but eloquent tales of the freebooter's exciting life, measures the scene with a look that means "how much plunder is here?" or turns, with the action of a wild cat, upon the running footman, who, preceding that stout Scindian gentleman in the brocaded cap, and padded chintz dress, has taken the liberty of pushing the knight of the road out of the way. There is a huge

* Confectioners. This description of the Shikarpur Bazaar belongs to the past times, when I first saw it. The palmy days of its commerce are gone by, probably never to return, and Kurrachee is now become the meeting place of nations in its stead.

† The long single-edged dagger used with such effect by the Affghans. It is about the size of the old Roman sword, and speaks volumes for the courage of the wielders.

mullah from Herat, an oriental friar of Copmanhurst, all turban, cummerband,* and brawn, looking down with infinite contempt upon the puny Scindees, amongst whom he has come to live and thrive. Fierce, bullying Pathans, stand chaffering with smooth-spoken Persian traders; Candahar meets Multan intent only upon preventing cheating by cheating; the tall turban of Jesulmere nods to the skull-cap of Peshin; and the white calico sleeve of Guzerat is grasped by the iron claw of Kelat. Here a greasy Moslem cook pours a ladle-full of thick oil upon a fizzing mass of kababs, whose greasy streams, floating down the bazaar, attract a crowd of half-famished Ryots to enjoy in imagination the pleasures of the table. There a Hindoo vendor of dried fruits, sugar, seeds, spices, opium, and hemp—the *tout ensemble* fragrant as an apothecary's shop in the dogdays—dispenses his wares to a knot of Jat ladies, with a pair of scales, and a set of weights, which would make Justice look her sternest. And there grim eastern Cyclops, blacksmiths, tinmen, and armourers, are plying their clanging, clashing, ringing trade, in an atmosphere of 150°, and in the

* A waistband; this and the turban are the clerical cap and cassock of Islam.

proximity of a fire that would roast a lamb. Yet heard through this din is the din of the human voice. Every man deems it his duty on 'Change to roar rather than speak; none may be silent, even the eaters of sweetmeats, and the smokers of tobacco, must every now and then open their mouths to swell the clamour floating around them. Except when two crafty Hindoos settle a transaction together, with their fingers concealed from public view under the darkness of a sheet, no one pice* ever changes hands without a dozen offers and rejections, a quantity of bad language, and a display of chapmanship highly curious to the Western observer, as showing the comparative value of time, labour, and bullion, in the East. Curious, but by no means pleasant. The eye revolts at almost every object that meets it, not excluding the human face divine diabolically contorted;—the ear is sick of the huge doses of din perpetually administered to it. Other delicate organs suffer from the atmosphere, which is stiflingly close, to use no stronger expression. The mats are by no means so efficient against sun and reflected heat, as the stone vault of an Affghan

* A small copper coin.

bazaar; and the clouds of dust, raised by the many trampling feet, render a quarter of an hour's stay here a very *pénible* part of an observant traveller's devoirs.

Before we go I must particularly point out to you the proper Shikarpur Hindoo, a small, lean, miserable-looking wretch, upon whose drawn features, piercing black eye, wrinkled brow, hooked nose, thin lips, and cheeks of crumpled parchment, Avarice has so pressed her signet, that every one who sees may read. His dress is a turban, once, not lately, white, and a waistcloth in a similar predicament: he wears the thread of the twice-born over his shoulder, and a coat of white paint, the caste-mark, on his forehead; in his hand is a huge rosary—token of piety, forsooth! and behind his ear a long reed pen. That man is every inch an Eastern trader. He may own lacs of rupees, for aught I know: I see he never loses an opportunity of adding a farthing to them: he could buy a principality, with a nation of serfs, in the hills; he cringes to every mountaineer who approaches his cloth stall, or his little heaps of silver and copper, as if he deserved and expected a blow from the freeman's fist. Scarcely a Moslem passes him by without leaving an audible execration upon his half shaven pate, and the long, ragged mustachios which droop over the orifice he uses as a mouth. There is a villainous expression in Shylock's eyes as the fierce fanatics void their ire upon his head and stubby beard, but nothing in the world would make him return insult for insult. Nothing but an attempt to steal one of his coppers, or to carry off a sixpenny bit of cloth.

Shikarpur appears to have been built about A.D. 1617. The position of the town, an eminently favourable one to commerce, soon made it the main *entrepôt* of the Khorasan and Indian caravan trade. The country around has been rich and productive, traces of this still remain in the large and numerous canals that intersect it. In A.D. 1786, the Affghan monarch, Taymur Shah, when he permitted the Talpur Beloch Ameers to succeed the Kalhora princes of Scinde, raised Shikarpur high above all the marts of the Indus, by privileging Hindoos to settle in it and trade, without fear of indefinite extortion. These people are principally of the Lohana and Bhatia castes, common in Scinde and the southern provinces of the Punjaub. Their spirit of enterprise, raised by such simple means, showed itself in a way that deserves commemoration.

The Shikarpuri, having few or no home manufactures, devoted his energies to banking transactions; and in less than half a century he extended his operations over the greater part of Asia. From China to Turkey, from Astracan to Hyderabad in the Deccan, there was scarcely a single considerable town without a Shikarpuri, or the agent of a Shikarpuri, in it. A traveller starting from this town you might, and in some cases you still may, obtain bills of exchange to be discounted in places distant a six months' march, without question or demur, and you may possibly owe the whole state of your neck or throat to the interested good offices of the discounter.

The rude instruments with which the Shikarpuri banker works, is called a Hundi: it is a short document, written in the usual execrable stenography, upon a square scrap of flimsy bank-note paper, somewhat in this form:—

1¼ True is the deity Sri.*

1. To the worthy of every respect; may you

* The invariable initiating formula: what the mystic meaning of 1¼ may be I cannot even attempt to solve.

always be in good health! May you always be happy! Mr. Brother Jesu Mal.

2. From Shikarpur, written by Kisordas; read his compliments!

3. And further, sir, this one hundi of 1000 rupees I have written on you in numerals and in letters rupees 1000; and the half, which is five hundred, of which the double is one thousand complete; dated the —— of —— in the year of Vikramaditya,* to be paid at Kabul, after the term of —— days to the bearer: the money to be of the currency of the place.

In the year of Vikramaditya, &c. &c.

There are private marks on the document which effectually prevent forgery and swindling, as they are known only to the writer and his correspondents. You may imagine, Mr. Bull, how useful a few bits of paper like these are, when you are riding through a region in which, to produce a single gold coin, would be the best arrangement you could make for securing a sudden death.

It is customary among the Shikarpur Hindoos, after receiving a commercial education, and studying

* The founder of a well-known Hindoo era.

the practice of trade at home, to marry a wife with much solemnity. When the first child is born the husband prepares for his journey, and after taking leave of his family most affectionately, he starts alone for some distant country, probably, with the intention of spending half his life there. Wherever lucre calls him he goes; among the fiery Bedouins of Arabia, the fanatic citizens of Bokhara, the extortionate Persians, the inhospitable regions that lie far beyond the "Houses of snow,"* and the rugged ruffians of the Hindoo-killing hills.† If favoured by Lakshmi he may attain affluence and considerable political influence in the land of his exile: his stores of cloth and jewellery, his powers of calculation, and his command of capital may raise him to be farmer of the revenue, in which position, his acuteness, and his comparatively honest conventional dishonesty may endear him, in spite of his creed, to the king or governor of the country. Otherwise he must content himself with picking the pockets of the fair sex, with cajoling the savages among whom he lives, and with scraping together by slow degrees, a little fortune, the pro-

* The Himalayas.

† The Hindu-Kush or Sulimanian mountains in Affghanistan.

duce of barterings and bargains by which he is invariably the gainer. Thus pass away the finest years of his life. He is easily expatriated, as is your family, Mr. Bull; and also like yours, he looks forward to a return home, consoling himself with the hope, not of laying his bones, but of becoming ashes like a good Hindoo, in his "fatherland." However, it very often happens that his home when he returns to it, is like the old Crusader's, scarcely recognisable, and that a sterner power than his will forbids the gratification of his poor wish about the ashes.

The fair sex at Shikarpur has, as might be expected, earned itself an unenviable reputation. The ladies are celebrated for beauty, freedom of manners, and the grace with which they toss the kheno:* their attractions often prove irresistible to the wild Hillmen that flock down to sell their horses, woollens, and dried fruits in the low country. You will see about the town more than one half crazy half naked beggar, who, once a thriving merchant, has lost his all by the fascinations of some Shikarpur siren. For such exploits these dames have more than once involved their lords in a difficult scrape, the Hindoos

* The ball.

of the other Indine cities having repeatedly proposed to place their northern brethren under the ban of the tribe till they can teach their better halves better morals.

* * * *

A considerable portion of the population hereabouts is of Affghan blood. They are probably the descendants of those warriors who settled in the country during the invasions which so rapidly succeeded each other of yore. Many of these are landed proprietors: the feudal grants obtained from the native princes being continued to them by our Government. It is impossible to mistake the appearance of these people. The men are beyond compare the handsomest race we have yet seen. Their coarse mountain skins and "rocky faces" have been softened down into delicacy by the heat and the comforts of the plains.—

Look at this magnificent animal with Grecian features; large black eyes, straight thin nose, short proudly curled lip, and chiselled chin; a clear brown complexion lighted up with a colour one might mistake for rouge, raven curls descending in masses upon his broad shoulders, and a beard soft, black, and glossy as silk. Can the human figure anywhere show a finer mixture of strength and symmetry, and perfect grace?

I never saw any of the ladies, but those that have had the good fortune, assure me that they are as comely after their kind, as is the ruder sex. Both appear to outstrip in intellect, as in physical development, the other inhabitants of the plains: many of them can read, write, and speak three languages; Persian, Pushtu, and Scindee; they yield to none in bravery and rascality, and they enjoy the respect of all, as being Bachcheh-Aughan,* "Sons of the Affghan," and, by direct consequence, they are haughty, high-spirited, and vindictive as superior race could wish to be.

* The Pushtu, or Affghan pronunciation of "Affghan."

CHAPTER XXVII.

UPPER SCINDE.—DURRANEE HEROISM OF SENTIMENT.

These few pages will be rather an account of what you did *not*, than of what you did see, Mr. Bull.

We have almost exhausted the beauties and the deformities of Young Egypt: nothing remains but inferior second editions of what we have already admired and condemned. Besides, the mornings and evenings are waxing tepid, the mid-days torrid, the simooms occasional, and the dust storms frequent. It is the season of the vernal equinox, that is to say, rank summer; spring never smiled on these regions. To which circumstance you owe your escape, sir, from many a long uninteresting ride, and many a long uninteresting description.

* * * *

A belt of productive, not producing, country girds Shikarpur; an expanse of jungles patched with wheat, holcus, and sugar cane. Beyond it all is a desert. Not a sea of sand, the desert of your imagination before you left England, or a rocky barren waste, the desert of your observation as you crossed over to Suez; here the desert is a dead flat—a horizon-bounded circle of dull, dry, hard clay, like the levelled floor of a mud house. It bears nothing save horse and camel bones; but although there is no more grass on it than in the streets of London or Paris, a little water would soon render it verdurous as the byways of Pisa, Warwick, or Arras.

If we were to visit Janiderah, about twenty-five miles from Shikarpur, we should find a wretched little village with a ruinous fort, a prodigious burial-ground, and a solitary tree which harbours all the birds in the neighbourhood. We might see the Beloch Gasparonis, half pioneers half pensioners, who inhabit this delectable spot under the charge of a British officer, whose throat they have not yet cut. Eleven miles beyond Janiderah is Kangarh, the head-quarters of the Scinde horse, an active body of irregulars, admirably constituted to protect a frontier of the kind. Should we turn towards the north-east, and journey still along the right bank of the river towards Kusmor, our ephemerides would contain something generally interesting in the following form:—

1. Rustam, eleven miles; three shops of grain, sweetmeats, &c.; forage procurable.
2. Bakhtiyarpur, twelve miles; village deserted, no water in the wells.
3. Gonspur, twelve miles; one shop, kept by a Hindoo Banyan, wells full, a dirty pond, houses numerous.
4. Banhar, eighteen miles; twenty shops, plenty of forage, no water except from the ponds, and that none of the sweetest.
5. Gobla, sixteen miles; ditto, ditto. Road approaches Indus through thick tamarisk jungle, here and there on fire.
6. Gehalpur, twenty miles; large village, grain and water abundant.
7. Kusmor, sixteen miles; a considerable settlement, with about twenty shops. Trade *nil* in this "port of considerable trade."

At Kusmor we should be on the northern frontier, a land which deserves for its blazon, "Snaffle, spur, and spear"—for motto, "vivitur ex rapto," as much as ever did those between Ouse and Berwick, in the good old times. Every little settlement has its "peel," whence the need-fire has glowed, and the slogan has sounded generation after generation: here Macfarlane's lantern tempts many a wight to the foray and the "kind gallows;" and as for "Hairibee," every clear spot with a tall tree upon it, has, some time or other, acted in that capacity. There men, armed to the teeth in spite of proclamations, all look like stark moss-troopers riding out to harry their neighbours' lands; and the women are—

> "Of silver brooch and bracelet proud,"

as ever were the dames and daughters of the "Limitanei." An unpleasant feature in the live part of the picture is the quantity of mutilation we observed. This gentleman has no ears, that lady no nose, one fine youth has lost an eye, and many a grim-visaged senior is unimanous,* unmistakeable signs that they have been engaged in, and what is worse, detected in certain lively little indulgences, against which the Decalogue has made special protest.

The villages in this land of robbers are miserable

* In the old times theft upon the Borders being considered march-treason, was invariably punished with mutilation.

collections of mud huts, straggling about the tall walls of mud forts, in peaceful times cattle-pens, at others proper dens of thieves. They are generally square buildings, with round towers at each angle, lancet-shaped crenelles or battlements to shelter matchlockmen, high parapets and well-defended gateways, which, in the hour of need, are built up with sun-dried bricks. Inside are the accommodations for man and beast, a well or two, heaps of forage and granaries — cylindrical earthen vessels eight or nine feet high, covered over and pierced at the bottom with a hole, through which the contents are drawn off.

You may like to hear, Mr. Bull, the approved method of attacking these wasps' nests, which are apt to puzzle a novice in military matters, as many a Brigadier Dunderhed and Colonel Ninny might, if he would, confess. The "old hand" commences with a demonstration, say 200 men, carrying sham ladders, firing their muskets, and making a noise that will certainly cause every soul in the fort to leave his post, and rush madly towards the supposed point of attack. This is the time when a man may steal to the gate unobserved, bearing a bag of powder, with a slow match lighted, hang it up by its hook against a convenient part of the beams, and "make himself scarce" as soon as he can. Success is now certain, provided that the enemy has not built up the gateway too well, that the charge is not so strong as to block up the road by throwing down the whole entrance; or that, on the other hand, it is not so weak as to do insufficient damage. Immediately after the explosion, three or four hundred bayonets, not *sabres*, whom Dunderhed is fond of putting in orders, start up from the nearest cover, tumble in over the shattered planks and blown-to-bits brick, effect all the harm they can, whilst the demonstrating party, hurrying round to the entrance, curtail the number of the fugitives. This, Mr. Bull, is a remarkably neat way, because whatever is in the fort—grain, cattle, and other things—falls into your hands.

"But why not breach the gate with guns?"

Because, in the first place, you may not happen to have any with you, and secondly, if you had them, the entrance is often so well defended by a quincunx of round towers, that you would have to batter down these first. Which "wouldn't pay."

If such an attack on the gate be deemed unadvisable,—a spy for instance informs you that twenty-five feet deep of brickwork have been thrown up behind it, —you may mine through the curtain readily enough by planting strong posts and beams, penthouse fashion, against it, and by supplying the workmen with pickaxes, and water to wet the clay. Your muskets must protect them against the matchlocks and arrows, spears and stones, hot water and boiling oil of the defenders, till they have dug about eight feet into the wall, when they lodge their powder, fill up the outside hole with bags of the excavated earth, light the match and bolt out of their hiding place, trusting, as brave soldiers often must, to their heels and Providence.

I suppose you to be deficient in "material," as you generally are in India on small occasions. Had you a few mortars you would shell the place inside out in half a day, and a battery of breaching guns would in twenty-four hours cut a square hole in the curtain sufficient to admit a pair of camels abreast.

* * * *

The Scindians in the north are far more warlike than their southern brethren: still there is the taint of timidity in their composition. Although they have brought themselves to bandy blows with the Beloch, and occasionally to beard the Brahui, they would generally rather run than fight, and huddle into their forts, than defend themselves in the field. Perhaps the Affghans are the only people in this part of the world who ever dared to prefer the wall of men to the wall of mud,—and that too, I suspect, only in history.

History deposits upon oath that, when Ahmed Shah the Durranee, proposed to encircle Candahar, his capital, with a moat and a rampart, his Sardars, or chiefs, vehemently objected to such precaution, propounding that their good swords were the monarch's properest defence. I suppose we must believe her. The tale is current amongst the Affghans, and a popular poet chose it as the subject of a Ghazal or Ode, which, Mr. Bull, I have ventured to translate for your fuller understanding of oriental Carmagnolery :—

Place not thy trust—
Great king—in rampart, fosse, or height of town,
Which are as dust
In the fierce whirlwind's grasp, before the might
Of man's strong mind !

The monarch throned upon the willing hearts
Of human kind,
The prince whose sceptre and whose sword command
Man's love and fear,*
May he not spurn the cunning craven arts
To despots dear?"

Indeed! A cut at Louis Philippe and the fortifications of his dotage, Mr. Bull! But allow me to conclude—

"Thy barrier be the steel-clad wall, whose crests
Are sword and spear;
Thy moat this plain—a vale of Death to those
That dare assail
The patriot king; thy tower of strength a name,
At which turn pale
Thy foes the bad, which as a sign from Heav'n,
Thy friends aye hail!
Such forts are thine, and long as these endure,
Fear thou no fall—
No guarded adit wants the lion's home,
Kandhár † no wall!"

* * * *

Returning to Sukkur and crossing the river, a few miles ride would take us to Aror or Alor, concerning whose ancient grandeur as the metropolis of Scinde in her palmy days, and whose dyke that is to burst

* Jamshid, the Great King of Persia, long since made a demigod, is said to have "ruled his kind by love and fear, always leading the good to hope, and the bad to despair."

† Candahar.

before the rolling wave of Hakro, I conversed at length some months ago; we should see nothing but a bridge about 500 feet long, a contemptible village and a ridge covered with ruins, amongst which a holy sepulchre or two are conspicuous, but uninteresting objects. Were we to direct our course southwards, we should after a fifteen miles dusty march, sight the gardens, orchards, and plantations, which surround Khairpur, the capital of Meer Alee Murad, the only remnant of the unprincely house of Talpur. There we might be entertained at His Highness's Timbuctoo palace, with a nautch, a battue, and a drinking bout—all of which, sir, I repeat, would now be tedious to you as a review of the events and descriptions that have passed in array before your eyes. Northwards along the eastern bank of the Indus, distant six days, lies Sabzalcote. I will spare you the mortification of it. You must by this time feel qualmish upon the subject of desert districts, dusty roads, tamarisk jungles, mud mausolea, lean Hindoos, puny Scindians, mosques, bazaars, and clay towns with tumble-down walls. At least, if you are not, I am.

CHAPTER XXVIII.

THE SONG OF THE BUNGALOW.—DOWN THE INDUS "HOME."

1st May, 184—Here we are, Mr. Bull, still sitting within our sundried brick box, on high backed armchairs of reed, with our feet *more Indico* upon the table, and glasses of pale ale *more Scindico* (it is 10 A.M.) placed within reach, on a floor freshly composted with one of the five venerable proceeds of the cow.* We have assumed a third variety of attire: this time we are neither European nor orientals, but an artful, though mongrel mixture of the two. Embroidered velvet skull caps surmount our shaven polls; shaven, because the happiness of life now consists in pouring cold water over them once an hour: instead of silk sheets and cotton coats, we wear muslin blouses—muslin, yet wet with transpiration. Wide Shalwars—wide to admit the air, and slippers without

* The Panjagaviya, as the Hindoos call them; if you want to know what they are, consult a Hindostanee dictionary.

socks—socks would make our feet feel as if they were being baked,—conclude our warm-weather toilette.

Pray sir, do in the name of Nostalgia leave off humming "dulce domum." If you wish for a song, let us spend one of our valueless hours in composing one expressly for the occasion, set it to a most original melody, and if you are that way inclined, sing it by fits and starts, with an interval for tiffin, all day. This is the season for fixity of idea. Many a man supports his mind through half a summer by means of a meagre pun, or some bare bit of slang, as "fin," for old fellow, and "peg," signifying a glass of pale brandy and soda-water.

We both begin with the refrain:—

We're sitting in our Bungalow
Lor how the Scindian sun does glow!

Then, Mr. Bull, as you especially are in the mood reminiscent, you will be pleased to continue—

Comes forth young Spring in gladsome plight,
With cloak of emerald sheen bedight,
While Zephyrs foot it deftly round
With joyous hours, all garland-crowned,
And on earth's warming bosom showers
Choice posies of the early flowers. *(A sigh.)*
The daisy dapples mead and dell,
And cowslip mixt with daffodil,

I scent the sweets of new-mown hay,
The freshness of the snowy spray;
I hear the distant village bells,
The lowing herds, the purling rills,
The soft bird warbling joyously
From blossomed bough and budded tree.

(*Another sigh at contrasts.*)

How lovely smiles the nascent day!
How brilliant her maturer ray!
How soft her splendours slow decay!
As slowly from the distant west,
Night rising in her sombre vest,
Appears to hush on silent breast
A drowsy world to balmy rest.

Stop, sir, you are merging into the deeply pathetic: there is a *ranz-des-vaches*-like twang in your intonation, a "Lochaber-no-more" look about your face which would paralyse the mirth of a subaltern's dinner party. Allow me to proceed with my "fytte."

I'm sitting in my Bungalow,
Like scorpion girt with living lowe,
In atmosphere rank, steamy, hot
As fumes that fly from witches' pot.
Above, the air is lambent flame,
Around, 'tis very much the same,
And what's beneath is fit to bake
With ease the biggest Christmas cake.
Instead of sweet May's pretty posies,
The smell of death * is in our noses;

* Let the man who wishes to understand the full force of this line, take up a handful of Scinde earth immediately after a shower of rain, and submit it to the action of his olfactories.

Where should be trees, and grass, and corn,
The fetid shrub and rugged thorn,
Diversify the scene forlorn.
Instead of distant village bells,
And soft birds singing in the fells,
The fire-wind howls, the jackall yells,
To living ears funereal knells.
The Stentor cricket screams his glee,
And corvus caweth fearfully.
"'Tis morn," (suppose) as we arise,
Alive, with looks of sad surprise,
We ask, indeed, as well we may,
What chance have we to live the day?
"'Tis eve," as prize-poem-poets say,
Half-roasted, parboiled, in dismay,
We make our minds to mete the mite-
like chance of sleeping wink this night,
A-writhing in our bungalow,
Like tortured souls in realms below.

* * * *

Verily an admirable opportunity is this of attaining the exact comprehension of obstinate King Pharaoh's obstinacy. You recollect, doubtless, what the plagues of Egypt were, although—you old heathen!—you have eschewed church these four times eight Sundays, and have generally conducted, or striven to conduct, yourself, "larkingly," as a Bow-street magistrate, making the most of a six-weeks' sinning trip to the "Continent."

As for the flies, and all the varieties of things with

vulgar names, you remarked that no sooner did the cold wind cease, than there appeared a swarm of "insect youth," so troublesome in their sweet infantine ways, and so large a family of them withal, that—

> "To us the goodly light and air,
> Were bann'd and barr'd—forbidden fare—"

—we lived in one perpetual gloaming, as a last chance of keeping the innocent little creatures out of our noses and mouths. Then wasps built in the doorways; and when we destroyed their nests, cut for themselves caves in the wall, whence they issue to sting us whenever they have nothing better to do. A centipede crept into your bed, a scorpion into my boot; luckily, I learned from an Oriental Sir John Suckling, never to draw one on without shaking it. The nuisance is now at its height. By day, gigantic hornets buzz through the rooms. By night, silent sand-flies sneak through the muslin with us, and angry mosquitos hum their complaints at their unjust exclusion from supper. We have, as you justly enough observe, other bedfellows, about whom the less said the better; that, too, in spite of boiling our cots regularly every second day. The boils and blains, like Broach and Aden boils, are not boils but ulcers—malignant ones, too, if they happen to settle upon your cheek or nose,—and the "prickly heat" makes you hate yourself almost as much as you do your neighbours—as you do everything in life.

We have no hail, but we have locusts—locusts and white ants—execrable animals, whose only office in the mundane economy seems to be that of providing the earth with finely powdered grey dust, at the expense of our books, our boots, our boxes, and our valuables generally. The grateful ground seems to breed them; in some places every step destroys a score. A tribe of American aborigines used, if I remember right, to eat them with fat clay;—could you not, Mr. Bull, make up your mind to try the taste? What a field for philanthropism! and conceive how immortal would become our names in Scinde could we teach her starving children to fatten upon a white ant diet! What did Ceres or Triptolemus compared with this?

Besides, there are large black and small black ants—insect bull-dogs, who allow themselves to be cut in two rather than relax the stubborn hold of their pincers upon our skins; large red ants and small red ants, social little beasts that delight in walking over the human face, nestling in the human hair, and hanging from the human moustache.

The cattle escape pretty well, but, *en revanche*, what with cholera and fever, dropsy and enlarged spleen, ophthalmia, dysentery, and congestion of the brain, our kind is happy and comfortable when in a household only the first-born dies. And finally, as regards obscurity visible, I ask you whether yesterday's simoom, composed of hot wind and black dust, in equal proportions, did not diffuse throughout our bungalow a darkness which, literally speaking, could be felt? O young Egypt!

To-morrow you must leave this place, Mr. John Bull; otherwise I cannot be answerable for what the French call your "days." I have ordered a dhundhi, or boat, to be made ready, and intend accompanying you down the Indus as far as Tattah, where—wide lands must stretch and wild seas roll, &c., &c.,—to be brief, old gentleman, we must say good-bye there.

* * * *

Have you all your curios, your treasures, safe and

sound? Your specimens of sugar and sugar-cane, your opium and hemp, tobacco and sulphur, your indigo leaves, your unknown dyes, your *échantillons* of cotton in every state, and your ingenious, but not original, essay upon the industry and productions of the country?—without which, woe to the traveller that returns! Your Tattah shawl, to be exhibited upon Mrs. B.'s shoulders, as a decoy for heedless listeners to stock-stories? Your isinglass, prepared from the lungs and air vessels of an Indus fish? Your "Bombay boxes," as the ladies call them in England—Scinde mosaic work of sandal-wood inlaid with ivory? Your cigar-cases, worsted-boxes, work-boxes, etuis and inkstands, cut out of the bhan-tree and covered over with successive coatings of contrasting colours, into which are punched grotesque and complicated patterns? The reed *fauteuil*?—it will make a capital chair for the garden of your suburban villa, and another famous tale-trap. The grass sandals worn by the people of the hills? Your dagger and signet-ring, with the "Jan Bool?" Your handsome posteen, and your embroidered leather coat?

We are now to go on board our dhundhi, where,

by-the-by, I have not neglected to lay in the requisite quantity of live stock, including the largest and fiercest tom-cat I could find. These vessels are tenanted by whole colonies of rats, and high jinks they hold when an unhappy stranger joins their party. By day they employ themselves in watching, with a predatory view, his goings into and his goings out of the cabin, occasionally running over the floor to test his activity, or walking up and staring at him to prove their impudence. At night they become more daring. They drop upon him from the boards above, race vigorously over his person, playfully pat him with their cold paws and sniff him with their damp uncomfortable snouts. If hungry, and in despair of finding anything better, there is no knowing to what lengths their unceremoniousness may lead them.

Briefly to describe the variety of craft* which we

* There are many kinds on the Indus. The jumptis, or state barges, used by the Ameers, were strong teak built double-masted decked vessels, propelled by enormous sweeps, and having pavilions at either extremity. The zoruck is the common cargo boat of the Upper, as the dhundhi belongs to the Lower Indus; it has no elevation at the stern, it is rounded off fore and aft, sails pretty fast, and sinks with prodigious facility. The kotal is a broad-beamed boat, used as a ferry.

Many other kinds may be found in particular parts of the Indus, where a rocky bank, dangerous rapids, or some such local cause requires a particular build.

have chosen. The dhundhi is a largish, flat-bottomed boat, with a high bow and even higher stern—a form good for enabling her to get off sand-bars, and to parry the violence of the shock when a bump upon the bank occurs. The masts are fixed upon strong beams resting athwart the gunwales: they can be raised and lowered at discretion. The sail is an oblong piece of canvas stretched between two thin poles and invariably placed behind the mast, so as to be used only when going before the wind. As we are to float down the stream, our fellows will assuredly not take the trouble to remove it one inch from its present position on the planks. The dhundhi is steered by a peculiar contrivance,—a perpendicular beam let down from the stern and joined to another projecting from the counter and rudder post. The former sustains the rudder, a flat frame of wood, like a fish's fin, prodigiously magnified, placed at least six feet away from the heel of the keel, so as to remove it from the little Charybdis that swirls under the stern of the old tub. This contrivance is worked by a complicated system of ropes and poles, one of which is grasped by the steersman's two hands in any, I should suppose, but a convenient way. On the whole, the outward appearance of the dhundhi is almost as barbarous and primitive as that of a French fishing-boat or an Italian felucca.

"Accommodations?"

There is a cabin which looks like a large cupboard thrown on its beam ends, almost horizontally: we may use it for a kitchen; we should find it difficult to accommodate ourselves in such a dining, drawing, or sleeping room. To guard against the vile designs of the sun, I have knocked up a kind of hovel of mat-work somewhere on deck. And being by no means desirous of drowning in this classic stream, I put the horses and horse-keepers in another boat, where they may amuse themselves with kicking and stamping holes in the bottom as soon as they please.

By day we progress at the uniform rate of six miles an hour. Part of this the current makes for us, part a pair of huge sweeps worked near the bow by two men whose activity I excite by the ordinary means—promises and cuffs. Regularly once a watch we ground upon a treacherous sand-bank, but thanks to the curvilinear construction of our craft we only spin round heavily two or three times, and slowly scrape off it into deeper water. This we occasionally vary by bumping against the bank with a violence which makes each one of the six hundred and seventy-three little patches of teak, mimosa, jujube, fir, and acacia woods composing the dhundhi, creak and grind against its neighbour with alarming violence. And sometimes we bring down a ton of earth, with a fall that threatens to separate the bottom from the two sides of our rickety conveyance. Although I by no means wish to make you nervous, Mr. Bull, I take the liberty of a "friend" to inform you that these craft, being fastened together by nothing stronger than bits of rope-yarn and bamboo-pegs, are in the habit of melting to pieces in the yeasty flood, and that, moreover, no one except a Mohana ever dived beneath the surface of the Indus and re-appeared with the breath of life in him.

To divert your thoughts from a subject never pleasant in anticipation, I call your attention to that Saracen's head which bobs up and down, frowning at the little waves, sputtering out monstrous sounds, and grinning at us with its white teeth like the friendly sea-beasts of which Arabian fablers tell. The fellow, however, is not an Adami-el-bahr, a merman, but a courier, who, finding it less fatiguing to float down the stream than to run along its banks, packs his despatches with his toilette in his turban, and commits himself to the safeguard of Khwajeh Khizr.* The gross material contrivance that keeps his head above water, is an inflated hide connected by two loops to the swimmer's thighs, and lying like a cushion under his chest.

Now you see in all its beauty the renowned way of Pullah-fishing,† a "piscatory pursuit," which, as a late traveller justly remarks, "more nearly reduces the human form divine into an aquatic beast of prey than any disciple of the gentle craft ever contemplated." The Mohana first places upon the water a buoyant vessel of well-baked clay, four or five feet in diameter by about three feet high, and shaped like a gigantic turnip, open above and flattish below. Salaaming to the river, and mangling an Arabic sentence, in which the name of Allah occurs, he disposes himself upon his float in such a way that the pit of his stomach may cover the aperture. He then strikes out with the stream, paddling with the action of a frog, till

* Chapter XXV.

† The pullah, called by the Scindees "pallo," is the hilsah of the Ganges—the sable, or black-fish. The usual weight is about two pounds, and the body averages twenty inches in length; the finest are found ascending the river as far as Bukkur, between January and April.

reaching a likely pool, he drops down deep into the water a pouch net attached to a long forked pole, with a checkstring to secure the prey when entangled. At such times he slowly heaves his net up, draws a knife from his girdle, settles the struggler's business, and deposits the corpse in the jar beneath him. To see the readiness with which the people perform this operation, you would suppose it, sir, to be a matter of little difficulty. Try it one of these days in some shallow place: you and your boat will part company as sharply and suddenly as your back and the Serpentine's icy floor ever met. The difficulty is to prevent the pot slipping from under you, like a horse's legs on a wooden pavement, or a platform of sheet rock. The habit of a life preserves the Mohana from accidents, although he passes half his days in the uncertain dangerous river. As the fish is always expected to swim against the stream, when the fisherman reaches a certain point, he paddles to shore, and carrying his jar on his head, walks some miles up the bank to recommence operations till he has secured sufficient for his day's consumption or sale.

I cannot permit you a dinner of pullah, Mr. Bull,

for this reason, that I never heard of a stranger indulging much in it without a retributive *colique;* moreover, the flavour is so undeniably good, that if you once begin eating it you will never leave off till repletion cry stop. Some travellers compare it to potted lobster, some to salmon, and some, profanely, to mackerel; others to fresh herrings: all agree, that in spite of all its bones they relished the rich firm *morceau* surprisingly, till they suffered for their *gourmandise.* The natives can eat it in any quantities and digest it, for the same reason that they can catch it and not drown. It is the roast beef and plum pudding, the soup and bouilli, the olla podrida, the maccaroni and polpetti of Scinde. Ask a Scindian what he would eat for breakfast? he replies, "Pallo!" for dinner? "Pallo!" for supper? "Pallo!" What his stomach loves most upon earth? "Pallo!" and what it mainly looks forward to in Paradise? "unlimited Pallo!"

En revanche, you may, with my full permission, and in perfect security, dine upon a sisar,* which our sailors have caught. You will find the meat very like that of shark—both might be imitated, for the

* A kind of alligator that lives on fish.

better comprehension of Mrs. B., by cooking steaks of what soldiers call "bull-beef," with alternate layers of stock fish. There is another chance for you, the bolan,* a kind of porpoise, and an animal whose flavour may be compared to that of a fattish pork chop dressed to pulpiness in rancid oil. Or I may be able to secure for you a cat-fish—so called from its screeching when drawn from its native element: to make another gastronomic simile, it resembles nothing but any bit of animal food which has been soaked in muddy water till it contains no other juice. If these delicacies suit you not, you may enjoy the sight of our crew enjoying them. And that spiteful little otter, their pet, who passes his days in concocting projects against our heels and tendons Achilles will, when we moor, supply us with a dinner of fishes, whose names are unknown to fame and to us, but which are not the less eatable for all that.

Our crew is divided into two gangs, and they work relieving each other about eight hours out of the twenty-four. As the wind is adverse, the cumbrous rudder has been unshipped to make room for a huge sweep, and the men are obliged to ply their oars vigorously to aid the efforts of the current. Every

* Baber calls it the water-hog.

evening, as the labours and heat of the day are over, we make fast to the bank, hurry on shore, secure fowls and vegetables, pitch our tent, and thank Heaven, that we haye not to sleep on board the dhundhi. We pass the night listening to the screams of the jackals, dozing and starting up at the loud reports of the frequent earth-slips.

This operation of nature deserves your attention, sir, as a kind of novelty to you. You are creeping lazily down the river when, about sixty or seventy yards a-head of you, from the wall of bank upon which the stream sets, suddenly starts up a cloud of dust, beneath which, big bits of silt and ragged bushes roll over one another into the water. In a moment, as if that were the signal, down comes the whole headland, a slice of ground some fifty feet long by forty high, and fifteen deep, cut out of the bank as neatly as if a knife had done it. Tremendous is the fall of the mighty fragment; the river's flank bursts to, and closes on it, heaving and roaring; our dhundhi pitches and rolls as it creaks over the spot; the boatmen look aghast at their escape: the passengers—being Englishmen—calmly delighted because excited. And passing on, we turn round just in time to see a tall mimosa half detached from its parent soil, trembling for a moment, then tearing away, by its weight, the long tough roots that tie it to the ground, bending, sinking, tumbling headlong into the depths of the stream.

Every morning, regularly as we start, we experience the usual little difficulty of mustering our crew and servants, especially the latter; and not before we leave one behind, to run wildly along the river-side for a few miles, do we succeed in introducing those habits of regularity and discipline which the soldier, the sailor, and the traveller should love. Off Sehwan we fall in with what we might expect, a furious storm, the precursor of the monsoon, which makes our lumbering boat run away with us over the water, transfers our thatched awning into the river, whirls half our lighter luggage away to keep it company, and nearly distracts our crew. Naval men have assured you that the Indus in flood is more dangerous than the most violent of Transatlantic streams: from what you witnessed of its prowess, at this early season of the year, you will not refuse it credit for extensive powers of mischief, when all contions are favourable.

Again, as sweeping past Hyderabad before a fair wind, which is fast brewing a cap full and to spare, our dhundhi, a good large mark on the exposed Jerruck Reach, is buffeted by the chopping sea, and pushed about by some half-dozen gales from as many points of the compass, as rudely as were the Macedonian's Triremes. Hereabouts a vicious-looking lahar, or rapid, runs half across the river, and by peculiarly Scindian management we float right into the black, and blue, and white-crested surges, that receive us into their enraged gambollings. "Dam ool Hakk!" (pronounce that first word "dawm," Mr. Bull, please)—"long live the Hakk,"* roar the sailors—"dam ool Hakk!!" They sink on their knees, blubbering and shouting louder than the raging wind. As old Hakk pays no attention to them, they have thrown him up, and are now promising a pot-full of sweet stuff to Lall Shah Baz,† if he will only enable them to cook it. Our Tindal—a reverend personage, with a stolid face and a long grey beard, the floodgate of whose eloquence usually turns upon two hinges—brief ejaculations concerning the power of the Lord, and long applications for causeless

* The great saint Bahawalhakk. See Chapter IX.

† Chapter XXIII.

bakhshish *—sits apart, as captains should, from his crew, and gyrates his extended forefinger with an air and a muttering, which bespeak a strong claim to salvage money in case we are saved. Our Affghan servants, men perfectly prepared to meet death in the form of a matchlock ball, or dagger, or even a few yards of cotton-cord, occupy themselves in diverting apprehensive looks from the yeasty waters, by meditating upon the advisability of throwing those howlers, the Scindians, overboard. The Portuguese, as is their wont, repeat the *ave* and the *credo* with a rapidity and a pronunciation that render them unintelligible to earthly ears; whilst you and I, Mr. Bull, screening our lighted cigars within our palms, are sitting upon the beams, which we contemplate converting into safety boats, with really a great deal—considering the predicament—of that pig-philosophy, which the old Greek so much admired.

* * * *

Here, at length, is the bundur, or landing-place, of Tattah!

It is evening. We have been tossed like the Trojan of pious memory, and like him we touch

* Largesse.

solid ground, with reeling heads and thankful hearts.

Our last dinner together !—

Own, old gentleman, that I have not treated you as a certain *compagnon de voyage*, whose habit it was in the morning to select a particular subject for reflection throughout the day, and to reflect upon it too, did me.—

Good-bye, Mr. Bull ; how I envy you !

Two days down the Indus—three more to Bombay; thence the last Indian voyage to the coal-hole of the East, and the Anglo-European baby-depot. Next the short discomforts of the desert and old Egypt, so delightful to the sane homeward-bound. Then the P. and O's noble steamer. And, lastly, to conclude the panorama passing rapidly before my spiritual eye, the joyful jump on English soil—the rail-carriage, second class—the cab—the knock at the door—the tumbling up stairs, reckless of box or fare—the falling into Mrs. Bull's extended arms—the proud look at Billy, who has grown prodigiously these last nine months—the huggings of all the dear little creatures that dance on your toes ecstatically—the first glass of London stout !—

Good-bye again, old gentleman!

*   *   *   *

He gripes my hand. He actually pulls out his "yard of silk!"—it 's after dinner, still!

He mounts the boat-side slowly, and waves his pocket pennant. His figure loses distinctness, diminishes, disappears in the distance.

Mr. Bull is gone.

And I remain behind upon this sultry shore, "alone!"—as novels will say—"alone!!"

How affecting (to oneself)—how romantic, and how *ennuyeux!*

THE END.

THE

STANDARD NOVELS AND ROMANCES.

Price Three Shillings and Sixpence each.

---

1. The Pilot—*Cooper.*
2. Caleb Williams—*Godwin.*
3. The Spy—*Cooper.*
4. Thaddeus of Warsaw—*Miss J. Porter.*
5. St. Leon—*Godwin.*
6. Last of the Mohicans—*Cooper.*
7. The Scottish Chiefs. Vol. I.—*Miss J. Porter.*
8. The Scottish Chiefs. Vol. II.—*Miss J. Porter.*
9. Frankenstein—*Mrs. Shelley;* and Ghost-Seer. Vol. I.—*Schiller.*
10. Edgar Huntly—*Brockden Brown;* and Conclusion of Ghost-Seer.
11. Hungarian Brothers—*Miss A. M. Porter.*
12. Canterbury Tales. Vol. I.—*The Misses Lee.*
13. Canterbury Tales. Vol. II.—*The Misses Lee.*
14. The Pioneers—*Cooper.*
15. Self Control—*Mrs. Brunton.*
16. Discipline—*Mrs. Brunton.*
17. The Prairie—*Cooper.*
18. The Pastor's Fireside. Vol. I.—*Miss Jane Porter.*
19. The Pastor's Fireside. Vol. II.—*Miss Jane Porter.*
20. Lionel Lincoln—*Cooper.*
21. Lawrie Todd—*Galt.*
22. Fleetwood—*Godwin.*
23. Sense and Sensibility—*Miss Austen.*
24. Corinne—*Madame de Staël.*
25. Emma—*Miss Austen.*
26. Simple Story, and Nature and Art—*Mrs. Inchbald.*
27. Mansfield Park—*Miss Austen.*
28. Northanger Abbey, and Persuasion—*Miss Austen.*
29. The Smuggler—*Banim.*
30. Pride and Prejudice—*Miss Austen.*
31. Stories of Waterloo—*Maxwell.*
32. The Hunchback of Nôtre Dame—*Victor Hugo.*
33. The Borderers—*Cooper.*
34. Eugene Aram—*Bulwer.* Price 5s.
35. Maxwell—*Theodore Hook.*
36. Water Witch—*Cooper.*
37. Mothers and Daughters—*Mrs. Gore.*
38. The Bravo—*Cooper.*
39. The Heiress of Bruges—*Grattan.*
40. Red Rover—*Cooper.*
41. Vathek—*Beckford;* Castle of Otranto—*Horace Walpole;* and Bravo of Venice—*M. G. Lewis.*
42. The Country Curate—*Gleig.*
43. The Betrothed—*Manzoni.*
44. Hajji Baba—*Morier.*
45. Hajji Baba in England—*Morier.*
46. The Parson's Daughter—*Theodore Hook.*
47. Paul Clifford—*Bulwer.* Price 5s.
48. The Younger Son—*Capt. Trelawney.*
49. The Alhambra—*Washington Irving;* The last of the Abencerrages—*Châteaubriand;* and the Involuntary Prophet—*Horace Smith.*

STANDARD NOVELS AND ROMANCES.

50. The Headsman—*Cooper.*
51. Anastasius. Vol. I.—*Hope.*
52. Anasasius. Vol. II.—*Hope.*
53. Darnley—*James.*
54. Zohrab—*Morier.*
55. Heidenmauer—*Cooper.*
56. De L'Orme—*James.*
57. Headlong Hall—Nightmare Abbey —Maid Marian, and Crochet Castle—*Peacock.*
58. Trevelyan — *The Author of "A Marriage in High Life."*
59. Philip Augustus—*James.*
60. Rookwood—*Ainsworth.*
61. Henry Masterton—*James.*
62. Peter Simple—*Marryat.*
63. Jacob Faithful—*Marryat.*
64. Japhet in Search of a Father—*Marryat.*
65. King's Own—*Marryat.*
66. Mr. Midshipman Easy—*Marryat.*
67. Newton Forster—*Marryat.*
68. The Pacha of Many Tales—*Marryat.*
69. Rattlin the Reefer.
70. Captain Blake; or, My Life—*Maxwell.*
71. Helen—*Miss Edgeworth.*
72. The Last Days of Pompeii—*Bulwer.* Price 5s.
73. The Bivouac—*Maxwell.*
74. Precaution—*Cooper.*
75. Jack Brag—*Theodore Hook.*
76. Rory O'More—*Lover.*
77. Ben Brace—*Capt. Chamier.*
78. The Vicar of Wrexhill — *Mrs. Trollope.*
79. The Buccaneer—*Mrs. S. C. Hall.*
80. Tylney Hall—*Thomas Hood.*
81. The Widow Barnaby — *Mrs. Trollope.*
82. The Soldier of Lyons—*Mrs. Gore.*
83. Marriage—*The Author of "The Inheritance"* and *"Destiny."*
84. Inheritance.
85. Destiny.
86. Gilbert Gurney—*Theodore Hook.*
87. The Widow and the Marquis—*Theodore Hook.*
88. All in the Wrong; or, Births Deaths, and Marriages—*Theodore Hook.*
89. Homeward Bound—*Cooper.*
90. The Pathfinder—*Cooper.*
91. The Deerslayer—*Cooper.*
92. Jacqueline of Holland—*Grattan.*
93. The Man-at-Arms—*James.*
94. Two Old Men's Tales.
95. The Two Admirals—*Cooper.*
96. Richard Savage—*Whitehead.*
97. Cecil—*Mrs. Gore.*
98. The Prairie Bird—*The Hon. C. A. Murray.*
99. Jack o' Lantern—*Cooper.*
100. Ayesha—*Morier.*
101. Marchioness of Brinvilliers — *Albert Smith.*
102. Belford Regis—*Miss Mitford.*
103. My Cousin Nicholas—*Ingoldsby.*
104. The Poacher—*Marryat.*
105. The Outlaw—*Mrs. S. C. Hall.*
106. The Phantom Ship—*Marryat.*
107. The Dog-Fiend—*Marryat.*
108. Adventures of Mr. Ledbury — *Albert Smith.*
109. Agnes de Mansfeldt—*Grattan.*
110. The Improvisatore—*Andersen.*
111. Romance and Reality—*Miss L. E. Landon.*
112. Catherine de Medicis—*Miss L. S. Costello.*
113. Percival Keene—*Marryat.*
114. Recollections of a Chaperon—*Lady Dacre.*
115. Experiences of a Gaol Chaplain.
116. Legends of the Rhine—*Grattan.*
117. Tales of the Peerage and Peasantry—*Lady Dacre.*
118. Sir Ralph Esher—*Leigh Hunt.*
119. The Hamiltons—*Mrs. Gore.*
120. Life of a Sailor—*Capt. Chamier.*
121. Hector O'Halloran—*Maxwell.*